The Emergence of a Musical Life

A Retrospective on Charles H. Webb

As told by Charles H. Webb

Inspired Forever Books
Dallas, Texas

The Emergence of a Musical Life

A Retrospective on Charles H. Webb

Inspired Forever Books™
"Words with Lasting Impact"
Dallas, Texas
(888) 403-2727
https://inspiredforeverbooks.com

Library of Congress Control Number: 2021905693

ISBN 13: 978-1-948903-54-7

Printed in the United States of America

Thank you to the team of editors:

Rebecca Chown, Nancy Webb Poole, Mark Webb, Kent Webb, Malcolm Webb, Charlie Webb, Wesley Webb, Abe Piedmont, Henry Upper

Disclaimer: this work is based on true events. Names, characters, businesses, places, events, locales, and any identifying details from incidents have been detailed in good faith to the best of the author's recollection.

DEDICATION

This book is lovingly dedicated to Kenda,
my wonderful wife of forty-three years.

TABLE OF CONTENTS

FOREWORD

"Your Friend is Your Needs Answered."
~Kahlil Gibran

"That man is going to be my friend." I remember it as though it was yesterday. It is what I told myself my first evening of choir practice when I found myself sitting diagonally across the chancel from the console where Charles, whom I had not yet met, was the organist and past choir director. A couple of short Sundays later at the break between services his wife Kenda came up to me and introduced herself. She warmly explained that she had four boys and a husband at home, and would I like to join in with them at Sunday lunch after the second service. I said yes. I didn't leave. And now, it's been a half century.

On that day, Charles and Kenda accepted and encouraged a slightly uncertain 19-year-old into their family with love and grace the way they welcomed countless others. After Kenda's early passing back to spirit, Charles continues this. Family is a component of the core that is music itself to us all but gifted differently in him. His counsel, humor, antics, and his certainty of path is true blessing. It guided me through a confusing critical time at university and let me know I was accepted fully in this chosen family. The effects of that welcoming gesture have been extraordinary and will continue to be as long as there is wavelength itself.

That of course, and the normalcy of it all. The relishing of cheap chocolate ice cream (a daily requirement), fast boats, old Cadillacs, kind embraces, and the most thoughtful words – this is Charles. Within these pages you will experience glimpses of his orchestration, his ongoing remarkable journey.

Thank you, friend, for a lifetime of Love, Light, and Laughter.

David

David Jacobs, friend, and honorary member of the Webb Family

INTRODUCTION

IN THIS MEMOIR, I HOPE to show the immense pleasure and gratification I have received all my life from music as well as the associations which made that life possible. From my earliest years to the present, the essential driving force throughout my life has been music, and music will continue to be the essential driving force long into the future.

I never aspired to be exclusively a pianist, organist, or church musician. My ambition was not mainly to conduct choruses or orchestras. Nor, at an early age, did I think of becoming a music administrator. Throughout my life, I had the good fortune to experience music in all these different ways, but always the strongest objective was to experience music in its purest form. Regardless of the benefits it unfolded to me, music has and always will be a constant learning process that shapes all aspects of my life.

In the pages of this book, you will read about the many people who influenced me, worked alongside me, gave me good advice, and deserve much of the credit for anything I have accomplished.

Throughout my life in music, two great and powerful forces supported me. In the beginning, my strongest support came from my parents, Marion and Haiz Webb, and my grandparents; Mattie and William Gilker, and Frankie and Roy Webb. Always fascinated by my musical talents, these individuals encouraged me daily. As you will see in the captions below, my grandparents lived across the street from each other, which gave them tremendous access to my activities and to those of my sister, Nancy.

4323 Vandelia, home of Will and Mattie Gilker, grandparents of Nancy Webb Poole and Charles Webb

4318 Vandelia, home of Frankie and Roy Webb, grandparents of Nancy Webb Poole and Charles Webb

Introduction

Neither Nancy nor I ever had a babysitter growing up. Our grandparents were always available, and when one set of grandparents tired of us, they sent us across the street to the other set.

Charles and Nancy swinging on the gates of 1603 North Garrett Avenue, the first house they lived in

My parents met for the first time when a car belonging to my Grandfather Webb rolled out of my father's driveway into my mother's driveway across the street. Fortunately, because the driveways were absolutely opposite one another, no damage resulted.

My parents attended the same elementary and junior high schools and graduated together from North Dallas High School. They both attended Southern Methodist University in Dallas, graduating with respective degrees in their chosen fields. Shortly after graduation, they married and began to raise a family.

With the help of grandparents, my parents provided me with a Steinway grand piano and a first-class education. I also had many mentors along the way and excellent teachers who made a big difference in my life.

Kenda, my understanding and generous wife, was my other major support. My brother-in-law, Foster Poole, always said that the person you marry either makes you or breaks you. He was certainly right. Kenda was my biggest cheerleader. Her unending support and collaboration in everything I did helped me all along the way. While I was Dean, she was First Lady. Graciously sharing our home with many friends, acquaintances, and colleagues, she served more than 30,000 meals by the time I retired. She also ran our household and reared our four boys, who also played a big part in my success.

There is no question that without my parents, grandparents, and Kenda, my life would have turned out very differently, and I am grateful for the inspiration that came in abundance from all those who played such an important role in my life.

PART ONE

The Early Years

CHAPTER ONE

Childhood and a Surprising Ability

I WAS BORN IN DALLAS, Texas, on February 14, 1933. My earliest recollection of playing music occurred at age four. Every Sunday after church,
I would go to the piano and pick out melodic lines of the hymns that had
been sung that day and play them on the piano for my mother. She thought
if I could do that without any teaching, perhaps I should have piano lessons.

The only piano teacher my parents knew was Elizabeth Gay Jones, a
well-known Dallas teacher. My mother had studied with her for a brief
time and found her willing to give me lessons. Luckily for me, she taught
in the Fellowship Hall in St. Matthews Cathedral, which was directly across
the street from our house at 1603 North Garrett Avenue.

I continued studying with Miss Jones until I was seven. Throughout that
time, whenever I was assigned a new piece, I would ask Miss Jones to play
it for me first. This enabled me to reproduce what she played on the piano.
Consequently, I never needed to use a musical score. Since the ability to

translate what is heard for the first time into music is not something that can be learned, my ability to do this can only be described as God–given.

At an early age, perhaps six or seven years old, after having studied with Miss Jones for several years, I was invited to play the piano at several downtown department stores that sold sheet music as well as instruments. In those days, no one had a cell phone, computer, or any other electronic means of playing music, and the only way to hear a specific song was by attending a live performance.

My grandparents were eager and proud to have their young grand–son featured at large department stores that sold popular sheet music. They would drive me to the various stores whenever my mother had other responsibilities, and I would play the requests of shoppers who wanted to hear their favorite selections. These were popular songs that I had learned to play by ear. Miss Jones did not work with me on music of this type.

Charles plays the piano at several down–town Dallas department stores

Charles plays sheet music for customers at the department store

One day Miss Jones suggested I audition for Dr. and Mrs. Paul van Katwijk. Dr. van Katwijk was a professor of music and Dean of the Southern Methodist University School of Music in Dallas, located just a few blocks from my parents' new home on Windsor Avenue in University Park. Paul and Viola van Katwijk were both brilliant pianists and magnificent teachers, and I was extremely fortunate to have the opportunity to audition for them.

The front entrance of 4005 Windsor Avenue, the house in which Nancy and Charles grew up

After I played a prepared piece (I regret that I do not remember what I played), Dr. van Katwijk put a piece of music on the music rack of the piano and said, "Now, Charles, play that piece for us." I sat there stunned and made no motion to play the music on the rack. I had no idea what the music was but it might have been an elementary piece from a graded instructional piano book.

My mother said, "Charles, didn't you hear Dr. van Katwijk? He told you to play that music on the music rack."

I sat very still and said quietly, somewhat ashamed, "I can't. I don't know how to read music."

This statement shocked my mother, but the esteemed doctor of music simply said, "Mrs. Webb, we are going to take your son as a piano student, but I can assure you that he will learn to read music!"

My mother had no further words until we were back in the car. I, however, had a lot of explaining to do.

In addition to teaching, as Dean of SMU's School of Music for thirty years, Dr. van Katwijk's responsibilities included locating and hiring outstanding faculty, setting salaries, determining academic promotions, and developing curricula.

As busy as he was, none of those activities stood in the way of his intense desire to see his music students succeed to the fullest extent of their abilities. He did not believe in having a teacher play an assigned piece before actual work began to learn it. I also remember his stressing again and again the importance of playing with loose wrists. Often students sat down to a keyboard and their wrists automatically tightened, robbing them of maximum control of finger dexterity and the beauty of sound.

There is no way to overstate the importance of the meaningful music lessons I received from these two geniuses. Throughout my grade school, middle school, high school, and college days, I had weekly lessons with both Dr. and Mrs. van Katwijk. They provided insightful knowledge, information, and inspiration sorely needed by me as well as other fledgling piano students.

When I was six years old, our grandparents invited our parents and Nancy and me to vacation with them in New York City. My Grandfather

Webb was an officer of the Federal Reserve Bank of Dallas, and one of his good friends, John Swan, was a vice-president of the Federal Reserve Bank of New York.

Unbeknown to us, Mr. Swan had arranged for me to audition to play on the Sunday evening broadcast of *Major Bowes Amateur Hour*. Radio was the dominant medium of the era, and this program was a regular feature on Sunday night radio broadcasts throughout the United States, similar to today's television phenomenon *American Idol*. Stars such as Maria Callas, Beverly Sills, Robert Merrill, and Frank Sinatra were discovered by *Major Bowes* when they were young.

To our family's great excitement, I passed the audition and was selected to perform on the upcoming Sunday broadcast. When we arrived, all contestants were seated at the front of the broadcast hall. Major Bowes assigned the musical selections we each would perform, and he chose "Home on the Range" for me, another piece I had learned by ear.

It was almost 10:00 p.m. when it came time for me to play. Alas, it had been a very long day, and I was sound asleep! Major Bowes, speaking over the national radio broadcast, said this was the first time in his long radio career that a contestant had fallen asleep while waiting to perform. Fortunately, I was roused out of my slumber and managed to get through my selection.

At the end of the program, when the audience was invited to grade the various performances, I was thrilled to come in second out of approximately twenty different contestants.

Nancy and I with our parents, Marion and Haiz Webb, posing for pictures after I played on Major Bowes' national broadcast in September 1939

In the 1930s, a favorite Sunday afternoon activity for families throughout the United States was to take an automobile ride; many of our Sunday
afternoons were spent in this manner.

*Frankie and Roy Webb, my grandparents on my father's side, with me standing on the run-
ning board of their 1936 Buick four-door sedan*

My parents, Marion and Haiz Webb

Headshot of my mother,
Marion Webb

Kenda's parents,
Tillie and Chub McGibbon

Another activity people in our community enjoyed was visiting the Hillcrest Mausoleum, a beautiful limestone structure located on the corner of Northwest Highway and Hillcrest Boulevard. Its expansive hallways and public rooms contained marvelous stained-glass windows that invited private discussions with family and friends, and its beautiful Aeolian-Skinner pipe organ could be heard throughout the building.

One Sunday, my Grandfather Webb spoke to Mr. Edwards, who managed the facility, about the possibility of allowing me to try out the pipe organ. Mr. Edwards kindly agreed, and after I played for more than an hour, he asked if I could play every Sunday afternoon, mostly hymns and sacred music requests from a large audience.

My grandparents were thrilled. For several years, I played every Sunday afternoon from 2:00 to 5:00 p.m. Because I was so small, the mausoleum staff modified the organ bench so that I could reach the pedals and still see the keyboards. I began playing these weekly organ performances at age six and by ear. I still could not read music at this time.

Charles, age six, plays the pipe organ at Hillcrest Mausoleum

Charles, age six, plays the Aeolian-Skinner pipe organ at Hillcrest Mausoleum

Charles, age eight, plays piano as Nancy and a friend sing

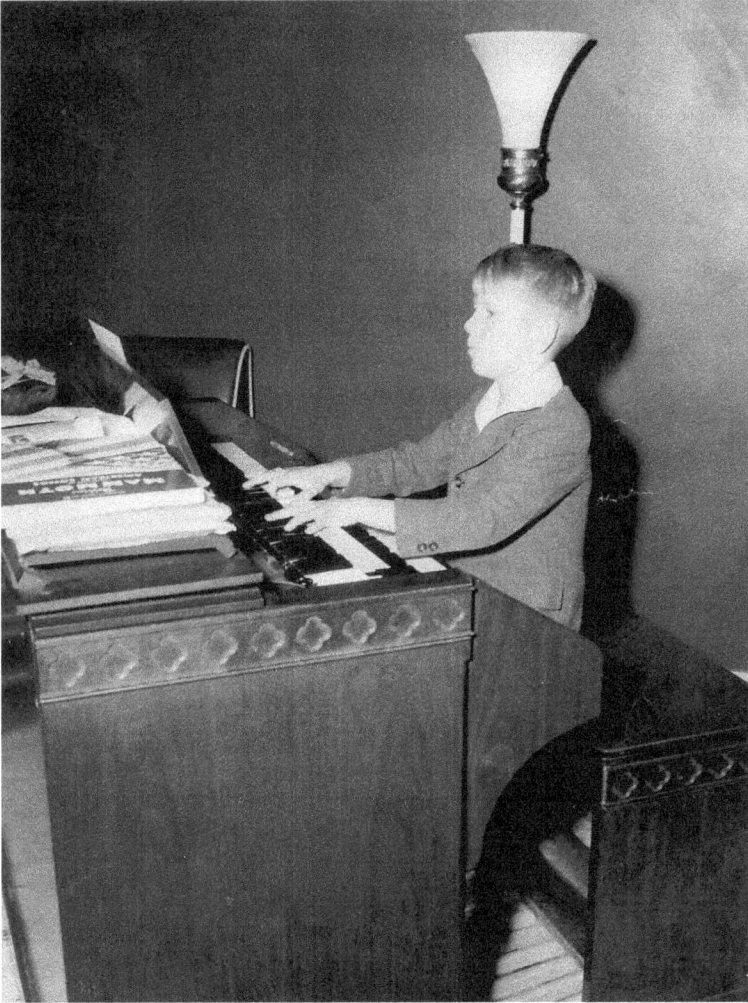

Charles, age nine, plays the Hammond organ at the Windsor Avenue house

All of this music-making was without financial remuneration, but a major benefit of these concerts was developing the ability to play without nervousness. I didn't know what a nerve was. Later in my life, playing a concert without feeling nervous was of great assistance in learning and performing in many different venues.

In addition to playing each Sunday afternoon at the Hillcrest Mausoleum, a number of opportunities became available for me to entertain at large parties. At that time, and perhaps still today, the idea of a five- or six-year-old child playing popular music in a concert setting was foreign to most people. The reproductions below of newspaper clippings, most of them from the *Dallas Morning News*, describe some of these events.

THE LUBBOCK AVALANCHE-JOURNAL

THE DALLAS MORNING NEW

SATURDAY, AUGUST 9, 194

Eight-Year-Old Dallas Youngster Pulls A Surprise On Hotel Lobby Crowd When He Gives Electric Organ A Good Workout

Charles Webb, jr., is 8, so
with some surprise to the
crowd in the Hilton hotel
Sunday morning when he
over and gave the hotel's
organ a brisk workout
prescribed by Bach, Be
ch and Mozart.
who had looked around
who would tell the child
organs are not electric
to push and knock about
their mouths and found
comfortable, closer stances
could listen to the concert
commenced.

No Organ Instruction

able to reach the pedals
Webb established himself
nist who with a bit of
on the organ could soon
to "ick out," as an organist
the fact he has had no organ
tion has not prevented his
mentation," which has
enough to find him play-
Hillcrest Mausoleum chapel
as twice monthly. Radio
announce the hour of his

music is characterized by
ed chords and no attempt
his experimentation" to
tricate runs, "but he shows
knowledge of music for
a musician in the au-

dience said.

Charles is a son of Mr. and Mrs.
Webb of 4005 Windsor street
in Dallas. He came here with his
grandparents, Mr. and Mrs. W.
Gilker of 4028 Vandelia, in Dallas
Gilker came to Lubbock in connection with the changeover from
manual to dial switching of South
western Bell Telephone company
slated for last midnight.

Charles began taking piano lessons two years ago.

"A lady asked me if I could play
the organ," he explained, "and I
went to a theater to see if I could.
I don't guess I know as much
about the organ as I do the

Organist, 8, to Give Concert at Church

Charles Webb, 8-year-old organ-
ist, will give a recital at Oak Lawn
Methodist Church, Oak Lawn and
Cedar Springs, at services at 8 p.m.
Sunday.

The young musician has made
many appearances in Dallas and
in other Texas cities, and has
played on a national broadcast for
amateurs. His program will be of
a semiclassical nature. He is the
son of Mr. and Mrs. C. H. Webb,
4005 Windsor.

The Times Herald

SUNDAY, DECEMBER 18,

METHODIST CHURCH TO HAVE CONCERT

Charles Webb will give an organ
concert at Oak Lawn Methodist
Church at 8 p.m. Sunday. He
will present a ten-minute program
of Christmas carols. Charles is the
son of Mr. and Mrs. C. H. Webb of
Dallas and has played the pipe organ since he was 4 years old. Rev.
John Donaho, pastor, will preach,
using as his sermon topic "Candle
in the Storm." At the morning
hour, his subject will be "Dreaming
of a White Christmas."

DALLAS WORLD
ALL-CHURCH PRESS
Trade-Mark Registered, U. S. Patent Office

DALLAS, TEXAS, AUGUST 8, 1941

For Youth Night Service!

Sunday night is Youth Night in Oak Lawn Church, and the service will be sponsored by the Young People. Beginning promptly at 8 o'clock, Master Charles Webb, seven-year-old son of Mr. and Mrs. C. H. Webb, will give a fifteen-minute organ concert. The Junior boys and girls will attend in a body, and the Junior Choir directed by Perry Bowland and accompanied by Charles at the organ, will sing. The regular choir, under the direction of Dr. Andrew Hemphill, will sing special numbers, and Mr. Donaho will preach. His subject will be "Forgotten Bundles."

At the morning hour, Mr. Donaho's topic will be "A Sense of That Which is Vital."

THE DALLAS MORNING NEWS,

SATURDAY, JULY 27, 1940

Child Musician
To Play at Church

Charles Webb, widely known over the Southwest as a child musician, will give an organ concert at 8 p.m. Sunday at the Oak Lawn Methodist Church, the Rev. John Donaho, pastor, said Friday.

The child has received recognition of his musical ability in the last few years through radio performances and appearances on college programs. He appeared on Major Bowes' amateur hour last year. He is the son of Mr. and Mrs. C. H. Webb, 4005 Windsor, and the grandson of Mr. and Mrs. R. O. Webb and Mr. and Mrs. W. M. Gilker, all of Dallas. His grandparents are members of the Oak Lawn Methodist Church.

Mr. Donaho will preach Sunday evening on Forgotten Bundles, and Sunday morning on A Sense of That Which Is Vital.

The Times Herald

DALLAS, TEXAS,

SUNDAY MORNING, JULY 28, 1940

TO GIVE CONCERT

CHARLES WEBB.

Charles Webb, son of Mr. and Mrs. C. H. Webb, 4005 Windsor, Dallas, will give an organ concert Sunday evening at 8 o'clock at the Oak Lawn Methodist Church. Charles has received widespread recognition throughout Texas and the Southwest. He appeared last year on the Major Bowes' amateur hour. The Rev. John Donoho, pastor, will preach Sunday morning on "A Sense of That Which Is Vital," and at night on "Forgotten Bundles."

DALLAS WORLD

ALL-CHURCH PRESS

Trade Mark Registered, U. S. Patent Office

DALLAS, TEXAS, FRIDAY, DECEMBER 27, 1940

Master Charles Webb, Oak Lawn's own "Child Organist," will give a fifteen-minute program, which will include a number of Christmas Carols. Charles is an active member of the Primary Department of the Church School, and is loved by both young and old in this Church.

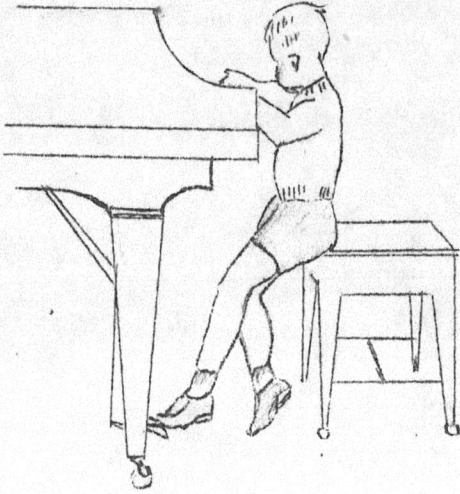

YOU ARE CORDIALLY
INVITED TO HEAR
CHARLES H. WEBB JR.
"THE FIVE YEAR OLD VIRTUOSO"
(GRANDSON OF W.M.GILKER, TRAFFIC SUPV.)
IN A PROGRAM OF
CHRISTMAS AND POPULAR MUSIC

TWELVE O'CLOCK NOON   THURSDAY
IN THE AUDITORIUM   DECEMBER 22, 1938

Throughout my childhood, music was the defining feature of my life, and though I didn't yet know it, it was going to stay that way.

CHAPTER TWO

My Early Association with Music and the Church

MAKING MUSIC IN THE CHURCH was a very important part of my classical career, and this association has lasted my entire life.

As a child, I was eager to approach the organ in my home church after services ended each week not because this organ was special but because it gave me another opportunity to practice my craft. With the approval of Annette Black, regular organist at Oak Lawn United Methodist Church, I would stay in the sanctuary after the worshipers had departed and experiment with the arrangement of stops and various dynamic possibilities.

Organist at 4 Plays at Church

A little too short to reach the pedals of an organ, 5-year-old Charles H. Webb Jr., 4005 Windsor, can play almost any request, and play it well. He plays mostly by ear, although he — a year. He has never studied the organ, but likes to play it, and will sit and play for hours, his parents say, just for the pleasure of hearing the music. He played at the Oak

—News Staff Photo.

Charles, age four, plays the organ after a church
service at Oak Lawn United Methodist Church

My formal instruction on the pipe organ was initially limited to a few lessons given by Dora Poteet Barclay, head of organ studies at Southern Methodist University. Ms. Barclay was a superb organist and played regularly for services at St. Andrews Episcopal Church in Fort Worth. Having studied in Paris with the famous French organist Marcel Dupré, she helped me enormously with the development of stop registrations and the unique technique required to play an organ properly.

During this time, around 1945, another outstanding musician entered my life. The newly appointed Minister of Music at First United Methodist Church of Dallas, Dr. Glen Johnson, bought a house next door to my family's home on Windsor Avenue. Dr. Johnson and I became fast friends, and he invited me to participate in wonderful music activities.

INTRODUCTION BEFORE MEN'S BANQUET AT

FIRST BAPTIST CHURCH, DALLAS, TEXAS

March 1, 1940

CHARLES WEBB

A born musical genius. The remarkable thing he has is not the result of teaching. It is his conception of harmony and the relation of chords. For his age, it is almost uncanny. His playing is not the whirlwind type, nor is it a memory of notes from a score. The harmony seems to run in his mind. As a result, he is never lost in playing his number, for he is not tied to any score. He might not play the same thing twice exactly alike. He has a sense of interpretation not found except in more mature minds or minds highly taught. His tiny hands cannot span octaves and, if he uses a piano stool high enough to level him with the key-board, his feet cannot reach the pedals, so he must partially stand. Apparently, there is utter lack of stage fright or self-consciousness. He is not a freak otherwise, but a hundred per cent boy.

He has an extensive repertoire, but instead of playing a long number, we are asking him to play extracts from several to show his versatility. Indicating his interpretation of sacred music, he will play, first, a verse and chorus of "The Old Rugged Cross."

(2) President Roosevelt's favorite,
     "Home on the Range"

(3) Chorus from Victor Herbert's,
     "Gipsy Sweetheart"

(4) Semi-classic song,
     "Somewhere a Voice Is Calling"

(5) From "The New World Symphony,"
     "Going Home"

(6) The old, familiar favorite,
     "Danny Boy."

Chief among them was a Sunday evening music program called *Chautauqua Sunday Evenings*. Broadcast from the sanctuary of First Methodist Church, the program featured a large chorus, symphony orchestra, and soloists who performed major music compositions from all periods and styles. Most of these performances required organ and piano accompaniment, and Dr. Johnson offered me the position as pianist for these exciting presentations.

Both the organist, Margaret Terry, and I were kept busy learning some of the great music compositions of all time. Dr. Johnson assembled a chorus of about 150 singers, and under his inspired leadership, the group developed into a disciplined ensemble that thrilled all who had the good fortune to hear them.

I enjoyed making music with Margaret Terry. Her skills at the piano and organ were of the highest level. As principal organist at First United Methodist Church of Dallas, she played a very large four-manual pipe organ, and she was kind enough to allow me to practice on that instrument. The diversity of sounds available enabled music of all periods and styles to be experienced from the console.

At age fifteen, I began my first position as a staff member at a Dallas church. Appointed as regular organist at Highland Baptist Church, my duties consisted of playing for two morning services and a 7:00 p.m. evening service. I also attended Wednesday evening choir rehearsals. Woodrow Wall was choir director, and he selected quality choral music that widened my knowledge of worship music.

Through my association with Highland Baptist Church, I met a singer, Louise Mackey Boynton, who had one of the most beautiful soprano voices I'd ever heard. Invited to perform at an evening service, she chose an imaginative solo, "I Talked to God Last Night," by twentieth-century American composer David Guion. The range and quality of her voice were breathtaking. For many years, we had opportunities to perform together, and each experience was a highlight of my musical development.

After carrying out organist responsibilities for more than a year at Highland Baptist Church, I received a call from Oak Lawn Methodist offering me the position of regular organist. Returning to my home church in this official capacity was an honor I could not turn down.

Oak Lawn Methodist Church

PART TWO

Education and Music

CHAPTER THREE

Southern Methodist University

I ENJOYED MANY MUSICAL AND academic associations throughout my high school years. I was honored to be a member of the National Honor Society, president of the orchestra, president of the Dramatics Club, and junior representative to the student council.

THE CORSICANA (TEXAS) DAILY SUN

May 11, 1950.

KINSLOE HOUSE'S TWELFTH BIRTHDAY IS OBSERVED IN COLORFUL WAY WEDNESDAY

By MRS. LYNNE A. WORTHAM
Sun Society Editor

Kinsloe House begins its twelfth year today with prospects for another successful season in which the facilities of the organization will be available for serving all phases of civic and cultural life in the community. Emerging at the end of its eleventh year with more than five hundred members and thirty-two affiliated organizations, and with a program that will interest its membership, it is highly appropriate that the clubhouse should continue as the center of women's civic and cultural activities in Navarro County. Kinsloe House is a living tribute to the dynamic spirit of its founders.

Entertainment Program.

As a prelude to the entertainment program in the Kate Whiteselle Auditorium, Mrs. Keen welcomed members to the twelfth birthday observance of Kinsloe House. She stated that it had been customary to present gifts to Kinsloe House each year, but that one of the most treasured gifts of all was to be presented at this time. At this point, she introduced Mrs. W. M. Forester, chairman of the fund raising project of the Piano Ensemble Players who had dreamed of a Hammond Organ for Kinsloe House, and whose dream, Mrs. Forester stated, had come true. "With the co-operation of generous-hearted citizens of Corsicana, we are able today to present a Hammond Organ to Kinsloe House," Mrs. Forester declared. "Without you, and you and you," she told her listeners, "the dream would not have become a reality." She further stated that the Piano Ensemble Players had sponsored the presentation of the second Steinway Grand to Kinsloe House five years ago, and that the clubhouse is now one of the best musically equipped woman's clubhouses in the state of Texas. She announced that the list of donors would appear in the Corsicana Daily Sun.

Accepted Organ.

After graciously accepting the organ for Kinsloe House, Mrs. Keen presented Mrs. E. G. Hall, president of the Piano Ensemble Players, who, in turn, introduced Charles Webb of Dallas, talented young musician who was to present a Hammond Organ program, through the courtesy of the Whittle Music Company. Mrs. Hall expressed appreciation to J. Howard Beasley of the Whittle Music Company who was in the audience, and gave facts concerning the accomplished young teen-age organist of the afternoon. The organ concert was an exciting musical experience for the two hundred members in attendance, and the young artist did not fail to justify the reputation that had preceded him. An engaging personality, admirable technical facility and the outstanding ease with which he handled the organ and its coloristic devices, all conspired to make Charles Webb steal the hearts of his listeners, who demanded numerous request numbers after the printed program had been concluded.

Young Mr. Webb's program was effectively contrasted, ranging from Bach to the Birthday Song (which was sung by the audience as a tribute to the clubhouse.)

The beauties of the Hammond Organ as a solo instrument were revealed to good advantage in the following numbers: To the Evening Star, Wagner; Now Thank We All Our God, Karg-Elert; Andante from Fifth Symphony, Tschaikowsky; The World Is Waiting for the Sunrise, Seitz; Prelude and Fugue in E Minor, Bach; Intermezzo from Cavalleria Rusticana, Mascagni; Largo from New World Symphony, Dvorak; Smoke Gets in Your Eyes, Jerome Kern; Londonderry Air, traditional; Ave Maria, Franz Schubert.

The organist made such a favorable impression with his listeners that they were reluctant to leave the auditorium, and crowded around the organ to hear his interpretations of their favorite numbers. And he seemed to derive as much enjoyment from the music as his listeners.

CHARLES WEBB

Dedicating a new Hammond organ in Corsicana Texas

In the spring semester of each academic year, Highland Park High School hosted a major music festival featuring orchestras, bands, and choruses from neighboring high schools. Each group was adjudicated by highly competent judges and then briefly performed for the combined groups in the auditorium. These choruses needed piano accompaniment, and I was chosen to be the pianist for these occasions.

JUST LIKE A WOMAN:
Young Pianist's Haircut Proves He's No Long Hair

By GARLAND MAC CULLUM

Charles Haizlip Webb Jr. has known local fame for about a dozen of his sixteen years.

You can see why when you know that since he was four, he has been playing the piano with all ten fingers and the talent that one ordinarily associates with a child prodigy.

Named Charles and, amazingly enough, called Charles by family and everybody else, the blond young fellow with the burr haircut now is well on his way toward being a first-class musician and the concert pianist that he hopes to become eventually.

But young Charles specializes in versatility. He doesn't have his hair crew-cut for nothing. Completely lacking in long-hair tendencies, the chap plays boogie as skillfully as he plays Bach!

The son of Mr. and Mrs. O. Haizlet Webb, Charles doesn't even remember when he first started playing piano. He has to listen to his family tell of the times when he was still in rompers and would come home from Sunday School, perch on the piano bench, and startle listeners with renditions of "Jesus Loves Me" and "Brighten the Corner."

His antics at the piano have amazed people ever since. Living next door was Miss Elizabeth Jones, a piano teacher, who began giving him lessons. Four years later he became a pupil of Viola van Katwijk, and when he was ten he began studying with Dr. Paul van Katwijk. He's still under the tutelage of the van Katwijks, who have guided him to such eminence at the keyboard that last spring he won first place in the district piano contest and placed third in the state competition.

Charles began his public appearances in the big time. When he was six years old, he played on the Major Bowes program in New York.

But the black and white keys on the piano aren't enough for Charles' lively fingers. He also stars at the organ. When he was six years old, he began a series of Sunday afternoon concerts of hymns at Hillcrest Mausoleum. At present he is assistant organist at the Oak Lawn Methodist Church and serves in a similar capacity at the First Methodist Church.

Charles gets in his piano practice on a Baldwin grand piano, a gift from his grandparents, the late Mr. and Mrs. R. O. Webb, who two years ago also presented him with a Hammond organ for home use.

What does this young fellow do for fun? Well, music is fun for him, the way he does it; but he has other ideas, too. He's great with a tennis racket and likes to swim a lot during the summer. He's just returned from the rodeo at Stamford, Texas, and now is back at the routine of keeping the yard and washing to car. As a sideline, he's also painting the kitchen!

Is there any other musical talent in the family, one instinctively wonders? The answer to that one is no. This future candidate for Julliard has a corner on enough musical genius to supply several family trees!

In 1950, the conductor of the combined choruses was Dr. Lara Hoggard, a nationally known choral conductor and staff member of the famous group Fred Waring and the Pennsylvanians. The Pennsylvanians toured throughout the United States and presented a television program that was watched by thousands each Sunday evening. I was introduced to Fred Waring by

Lara Hoggard, and as you will soon see, my association with Mr. Waring would go on to play a huge part in my musical career.

After finishing Highland Park High School in 1951, I continued my education at Southern Methodist University (SMU) with Dr. van Katwijk. I desperately wanted to major in music and discussed this dream with my parents. I was greatly surprised and disappointed when my father interjected, "A business degree is what you will need, and the banking profession is an excellent choice. Sign up to be a business student. You've played the piano since you were four years old and you can always play the piano, but you need to make a living, and banking is a fine career for you."

Well, I was not a rebellious son and I had tremendous respect for my parents and their judgement. Since my father was so emphatic, I enrolled at SMU as a business student and began attending classes in business law and accounting. However, I did not like these classes and spent considerable time wondering how I was going to complete this degree. Although I continued to play the piano, I wasn't able to practice as much as I wanted to, which made me very sad.

Just when I was beginning to resign myself to earning a business degree, I had an experience that changed my life.

The most important building on the SMU campus is Dallas Hall, a beautiful Georgian structure more than one hundred years old

In the spring of my sophomore year at SMU, I received a telephone call from Dr. Hoggard. He was calling to tell me that Fred Waring was going to be the chief clinician for a series of choral workshops that coming summer and that the person who had been chosen as accompanist had been drafted into the army. Mr. Waring was in a bind, and Dr. Hoggard wanted to know if I could be available to tour for eight weeks and play the piano for the eight choral workshops. There was no time for a formal audition. They would send me an airline ticket and I would fly to New York to begin playing. If Mr. Waring was satisfied with my work, I would spend the summer performing with him. If not, they would provide another plane ticket and I would fly back to Texas. Was I willing to accept these arrangements?

Fred Waring
with Charles Webb

On the right, posed familiarly, is Fred Waring, who will arrive in Dallas early Sunday morning to conduct the Chautauqua interracial program Sunday evening at First Methodist Church. . . . On the left, reading top to bottom, are Craig Timberlake, basso; Frank Davis, bass-baritone, and Charles Webb, organist, who will be featured performers in "God's Trombones."

Mr. Waring to Direct Choruses in New Work

Fred Waring, the famed choral director, will arrive in Dallas early Sunday morning from his Pennsylvania workshop retreat at Shawnee to appear as conductor Sunday evening at First Methodist Church.

Featured performers Sunday evening will include two Dallasites, Craig Timberlake, basso, and Charles Webb, organist, Frank Davis, bass-baritone, and Grace Nedra Perkins, soprano. Tim-

tesy of WFAA-TV, Channel 8, and the Adlета Company. TV sets will be placed in the church's large dining room and class rooms to accommodate some 1,000 extra patrons. The program will begin at 7:20 p.m. with the film featurette "As the Twig Is Bent," although only the performance of "God' Trombones" will be televised.

WARING, who is equally noted as a leader in the field of race re-

I certainly was. I felt I would be able to satisfy Mr. Waring, and I was willing to take the chance. Sure enough, both Dr. Hoggard and Mr. Waring approved of my work, and the experience of playing for these two fantastic musicians for an entire summer was a once-in-a lifetime opportunity. This was an incredible period of time learning and performing under truly ideal circumstances when I was not yet twenty years old. What I learned has stayed with me for the rest of my life, and I shall be eternally grateful to Dr. Hoggard for the confidence he placed in a young college sophomore pianist.

Known throughout the country as a superb training ground for conductors and trainers of choral conductors, Mr. Waring's summer choral workshops emphasized techniques to improve rhythm, diction, intonation, and other facets of choral singing. Approximately two hundred conductors from all over the country studied each week with Mr. Waring and his associates, including Lara Hoggard, Mr. Waring's assistant conductor. These individuals made up a choir that studied five to six hours each day. Mr. Waring drilled them intensely, and by the end of the week, the results were astounding. They truly sounded like a well-trained professional chorus. The opportunity to spend eight weeks in such a musical environment was an honor, and it showed me what could be accomplished with superior training and dedicated musicians striving to achieve the highest possible level.

During that first summer I spent with Mr. Waring, we traveled from the University of New Hampshire to Idlewild, California. I was one of two pianists responsible for accompanying all the sessions while he gave his one-week seminars in choral conducting. Toward the end of the summer, I asked Fred Waring if he thought I could be successful with a career in music. His enthusiasm filled me with hope.

Although my parents were happy and supportive of my summer activities, my father continued to stress the importance of a business career and the necessity of earning a living so that I could one day support a family. Summoning all my courage, I explained the situation with my father to Mr. Waring and asked him if he would be willing to talk with my father and express his opinion that I had what it took to develop a successful career in music.

It just so happened that one of the choral workshops that summer was at the University of Colorado in Boulder where my sister, Nancy, was taking a summer art class. While growing up, our family had regularly vacationed in Estes Park, Colorado, during the month of August. That year, my parents traveled to Estes Park and attended our concert in Boulder as guests of Mr.

Waring. Following the concert, without telling me he was going to do so, Mr. Waring spoke with my father.

Upon my return to Dallas at the end of that summer, my father told me about their conversation. He concluded, "If Fred Waring believes you can have a successful career in music, we will be fully supportive."

The next morning, I was in the Registrar's Office changing my major from business to music with an emphasis in piano performance. For the next several summers, I served as pianist for all of the Waring choral workshops under such luminaries as Fred Waring, Robert Shaw and Fiora Contino.

In the summer of 1953, when I was twenty years old, I met Wallace Hornibrook, one of the pianists for Fred Waring and the Pennsylvanians. My friendship with Wally blossomed into a meaningful professional relationship, and we played numerous concerts literally all over the world.

Wally and I soon discovered that we both loved two-piano playing. Whenever we got together to rehearse or perform, it was a great experience for both of us. Successfully playing two-piano literature requires not only two skilled pianists but also musicians who think alike and feel the music together. We were so fortunate to approach the pianos with singleness of mind, which made rehearsing and performing a great pleasure.

During the next fifty years, Wally and I played countless concerts in many different venues all over the world. A highlight was a month's tour in Australia where we played fifteen concerts, some with orchestra, and explored a wide range of two-piano literature.

We played our first real concert together the summer of 1953 at the University of Wisconsin in Madison. I discovered a copy of that program in 2001, and we decided it would be great fun to play the exact same program fifty years later to the date. Unfortunately, that event was not to be. On the fiftieth anniversary of that occasion, I played the organ for Wally's funeral. He had suffered a severe heart attack just days before the scheduled event. His untimely death was a shock and huge loss. However, I will never forget the joy and deep satisfaction of making music with Wallace Hornibrook. It will stay with me for the rest of my life.

Another pianist with great skill in two-piano playing was Marjorie Poole. A faculty member of SMU Music School, she was the number one choice for accompanying most students and faculty playing chamber music recitals. She also loved to play two-piano literature and had two pianos in her living room specifically for this purpose. We played many concerts together, and it was a red-letter day in the Webb household when Mrs. Poole's son, Foster, asked my sister, Nancy, to marry him. Now we had even more reasons to be together. There were many occasions when we enjoyed an evening of meaningful conversation, fine food, and beautiful two-piano music. Until her untimely death, Marjorie and I made music together as often as possible.

One of the most fulfilling aspects of my undergraduate university life was my membership in Phi Delta Theta, a social fraternity I pledged as a freshman and continue in today as an alumnus. The friends I made during those formative years remain with me, and I am grateful for such enduring relationships. I was honored to serve as president, another experience that will remain with me always, as will a not-so-uplifting incident that took place several years later in Bloomington, Indiana, while I was province president. In fact, I resigned my position immediately after this incident took place because I did not have time to deal with such mundane matters.

The fraternity was celebrating its spring social bash and wanted a large supply of cut flowers for the occasion. The pledges were ordered to find these flowers, and someone had the bright idea of taking them from a fresh gravesite. They found one at a local cemetery and loaded the flowers into the back of a station wagon owned by one of the pledges.

On the way back to the fraternity house, a policeman noticed the flowers protruding from the back door of the station wagon and stopped the boys to inquire what they were doing. They told the policeman they had just visited a peony farm and had purchased the flowers there. The policeman ordered the boys to open the back of the station wagon for him to inspect, where he discovered a casket blanket with "Good-bye, Uncle Walter," spelled out in fresh flowers. It was pretty difficult for the fraternity boys to continue pleading their innocence. Needless to say, by the time they paid fines and punitive damages to the family, they probably could have built a small greenhouse on the back of the fraternity house.

Death has now robbed us of some of our most cherished members, but we press on, knowing there are still memorable days ahead to enjoy the love we share. I am honored to include a letter to me signed by all the active members of the fraternity in 1955.

TEXAS DELTA
PHI DELTA THETA
SOUTHERN METHODIST UNIVERSITY
DALLAS, TEXAS

May 9, 1955

Mr. Charles H. Webb
4005 Windsor
Dallas, Texas

Dear Charles:

As you are about to finish work here and go into the Air Force, your fraternity would like for you to know how very much we appreciate you and the high esteem we hold for you.

You have set a high example for us, and have given of yourself, not only for the good of the fraternity as a whole, but each of us feels your keen personal interest in us as individuals. No matter how busy you have been, you have somehow found time for us. We are proud, too, of your civic and religious accomplishments and for everything you stand.

Please know that the thoughts of your brothers in Phi Delta Theta are always with you. We will follow your success in the future with genuine pride and enthusiasm born of your unselfish interest in us.

Yours in the Bond,

Letter with the signatures of all members
of Phi Delta Theta, 1955

TEXAS DELTA
PHI DELTA THETA
SOUTHERN METHODIST UNIVERSITY
DALLAS, TEXAS

April 23, 1955

Dear Charles,

To you on this wonderful day —in honor of you — I wish to extend my congratulation and also my appreciation for all you have meant to your community, to your church, school, fraternity, to my family, and to me.

That's quite a list, but believe me you have won a position of highest honor and respect in each of them.

You have been a wonderful example and a source of inspiration to countless people, including me.

Thank you for all you've done, for the way you've lived, and for the promise of wonderful things to come in the lives of many through you.

Best wishes always
Your little bud
Kent

Kent Beasley became my "little brother" in our college fraternity and our strong friendship continues to this day

Kenda and Charles with Kent Beasley

I enjoyed life as a college student. Foster Poole, my future brother-in-law, lived one block west of us on Windsor Parkway. Since Nancy and I often went to SMU in my car, we always saved an extra space for Foster. One particular day as we were driving east on McFarlin Blvd., we saw Foster walking toward SMU. We offered him a ride, and he readily accepted. Since we were late for our classes, I was driving over the speed limit. Reaching our destination, I jumped out of the car and raced toward my classroom in Dallas Hall. Unfortunately, a police car was pulling up behind me, its lights flashing.

"Who's the driver of this car?" the policeman yelled. Foster answered, "There he goes into that building!" and pointed to Dallas Hall. The policeman looked, shrugged, and with a pained expression on his face, slowly walked away. A moment later, he turned around and told Foster and Nancy that if it happened again, he would write them a ticket for speeding. Nancy and Foster were very thankful he did not ticket them since they still had to park the car and get to class. Oh, to be young again!

Dr. and Mrs. van Katwijk retired at the end of the 1954 academic year, and SMU made a superb appointment in bringing Dr. Orville J. Borchers on board as dean of SMU's school of music. He was also an excellent conductor, and I had the good fortune to serve as pianist for many of his rehearsals and performances with the Choral Union. As you will see, he became an invaluable advisor, mentor, and friend.

During my senior year at SMU, I studied piano with Gyorgy Sandor, a brilliant Hungarian pianist who had studied with Bela Bartok at the Liszt Academy in Budapest. Sandor was a world-renowned pianist, and I was fortunate to study with such an internationally acclaimed artist.

I loved my time at SMU and was very proud to graduate in 1955 with both bachelor's and master's degrees in music.

Dr. Willis Tate, president of SMU, congratulates Charles upon his graduation from the university in June of 1955

CHAPTER FOUR

The Air Force

FOLLOWING MY GRADUATION FROM SMU and having completed the four year ROTC program, I entered the United States Air Force as a second lieutenant and was stationed at Webb Air Force Base in Big Spring, Texas, for the next two years.

Driving west from Dallas to Big Spring, as the trees grew shorter and the tumbleweeds higher, I wondered what my future would hold.

To my surprise and joy, shortly after arriving in Big Spring, music again became an integral part of my life. Dr. Jordan Grooms, the minister of First Methodist Church in Big Spring, had been an assistant at Oak Lawn Methodist Church in Dallas. He knew our family and had learned from my mother that I was coming to Big Spring for a two-year stint in the Air Force and that I would be attending church services on Sundays.

Several weeks later, I was contacted by the choir director of First Methodist wanting to know if I would play the Christmas portion of Handel's *Messiah* with their choir at the annual church Christmas program. I was happy to do that, and rehearsals began in earnest shortly thereafter. This performance was a milestone for the Big Spring choir, and I had the pleasure of accompanying a number of subsequent major choral works.

While serving in the Air Force, I also organized a male chorus of pilots who enjoyed singing and had been in choral groups as undergraduates. When word spread that such an organization was forming at Webb Air Force Base, twenty-five or thirty singers promptly showed up for the first rehearsal. They were enthusiastic, willing to work hard, and exhibited excellent musical talent. After several weeks together, I asked the colonel who was in charge of the base if we could present a program of varied choral music in an evening concert. He was enthusiastic about the idea and arranged a date, time, and some advertising about the forthcoming event. When the success of that venture got around, we received several invitations to appear at neighboring bases.

One afternoon, Colonel Young, the base commander, called to inform me he had heard about a competition being held in the next several weeks for choruses trained on Air Force bases around the world. We entered the competition by submitting a tape recording of thirty minutes of music to an address in Washington, D. C. Several weeks later, we received notification that we had been awarded second place in the worldwide choral competition.

We were thrilled, and Colonel Young touted our victory far and wide. More requests for public appearances by the Webb Air Force Base Choraleers came to the base than we could possibly accommodate. It was a heady time for the singers, the base commander, and for me as well.

One of the former members of the Choraleers, Jim Marlin, recently wrote a book titled *On the Other Hand*. Below, I quote several paragraphs that describe Jim's experience singing with the group.

> Most of the singing I did came as a result of a young first lieu-tenant who was assigned as permanent party at Webb. Charlie was an outstanding musician who organized a group called the Webb Choraleers. It was one of the best singing groups I have ever been involved with, primarily because of Charlie. He was a fantastic pianist and organist and could direct either one while accompanying. (I later heard him on the concert stage as a solo and dual pianist and met him again in 1994 at the University of Indiana where he was just completing his twenty-fifth year as the dean of that prestigious school of music.)

In October, the Choraleers went on a trip to Dallas where we sang concerts at the Texas State Fair, at the First Presbyterian Church in downtown Dallas, and in one of the black high schools in town. We sang a Roy Ringwald cantata, the "Song of America," a patriotic number using American poetry and tracing the growth of the United States from before the Pilgrims to the Civil War. Ringwald was an arranger for Fred Waring. I thought the number was great, but I have never heard it done since then.

I also sang in a quartet associated with the Choraleers. We did a parody of the quartet from *Rigoletto* – the music was the same; the words were different. As an aside, three years ago, I was waiting for an audition for a small choral group in Boulder and was talking with several men who were also there for the audition. Somehow it came up in the conversation that I had been in the Air Force. One of the other men indicated that he had been as well. He asked where I had gone to pilot training and I told him Webb. He was an instructor there at the same time I was there. He asked if I had heard of the Webb Choraleers. I told him I had sung in the group. He then mentioned that he had sung in a quartet that had sung a takeoff on *Rigoletto*. I told him I was the bass. He was the first tenor. It seems that both of us had aged a little bit. That was really a small–world experience.

During the fall of 1955, another contact came to me from Mrs. K. H. McGibbon, a member of the church in Big Spring and program chairman for the Hyperion Club, a book study group to which she belonged. She had been told by the minister (who had forgotten to tell me) that I would probably be happy to present a Christmas program for her club. A date was set, and I showed up at her house at the appointed hour.

After the program, Mrs. McGibbon invited me to have supper at their home. For the first time, I laid eyes on a stunningly beautiful girl, Kenda, who was seventeen years old and the oldest of her three daughters.

Little did I know that I had just met the girl I would marry who would make me deliriously happy. Kenda attended SMU for two years while I completed my last year in the Air Force and spent one year as an assistant to Dr. Borchers at SMU. We were married at First United Methodist Church in Big Spring, Texas, in June of 1958.

The McGibbons held a beautiful reception for us around the swimming pool in their backyard. We had invited Fred Waring to the wedding, and though he was unable to attend, an interesting situation developed during the reception. One of our guests was Paul Waring, Fred's twelve-year-old son, whom I had gotten to know during the summer workshops in Pennsylvania. Suddenly, we realized Paul was missing. After a thorough search of the grounds and house, he turned up in the living room, where he had been having delightful conversations with several of the guests.

During my active time with the Air Force, I stayed in contact with Dr. Borchers. One day toward the end of my two-year stint, he called and asked if I'd thought about my musical activities and future beyond being discharged from the Air Force. The truth was, I had not. His inquiry brought it to the forefront of my mind, so I asked Dr. Borchers if he had any words of wisdom for me. He told me he thought I should give serious consideration to continuing my education to obtain a Doctor of Music degree. He then said that Indiana University (IU) was the place to go.

He was especially enthusiastic about IU's doctoral piano program and spoke of several faculty currently teaching in Bloomington. Because SMU did not offer a doctorate in music at that time, it seemed reasonable to accept Dr. Borchers' suggestion. I also accepted his offer to work as an assistant in his office for one year. At the end of that academic year, I applied to the Indiana University School of Music graduate program, was accepted, and enrolled that very week for the 1958 fall semester.

One evening while Kenda and I still lived in Dallas, we were entertained by Charles Meeker, the director of the state fair musicals. We drove to the auditorium with Nancy and her husband, Foster, and thoroughly enjoyed the performance. Afterwards, totally enraptured by the performance and the fact that we were newlyweds and deeply in love, we drove home.

Upon our arrival, my mother asked, "Where are Nancy and Foster?" To our horror, we realized we had completely forgotten them. They ended up walking to the police station to call home. By the time Kenda and I returned to the auditorium to get them, most of the lights at Fair Park had been turned off. To make matters worse, we were driving Foster's car. Needless to say, we took quite a bit of ribbing for this incident.

CHAPTER FIVE

Early Years at Indiana University

KENDA AND I MOVED TO Bloomington in 1958 and entered Indiana University School of Music that fall. I was beginning my doctorate in piano performance and Kenda was completing a bachelor's degree in her chosen field of music therapy.

Dr. Borchers had recommended the doctorate in performance if I wanted more advanced study before embarking on a music career. I knew at that point that my career would entail teaching or performance or a combination of both, and I very much felt I needed additional study. Beyond a master's degree, there were very few opportunities to study performance in advanced degree programs. When I entered the program at Indiana University, approximately ten schools, all in the United States, offered performance doctorates.

At that time, music study was traditionally based on European models prominent from the eighteenth through the mid-twentieth centuries. Private study of the instrument or voice and conservatory training were the primary means of educating the most gifted students, who were clearly destined for solo or orchestral careers. In the conservatory, the primary teacher gave all the instruction on the instrument. Perhaps a nominal course in music theory and literature was offered. A study of music theory and literature or composition was offered at some major universities in doctoral programs, but there was no performance element.

The performance doctorate I was entering was entirely different, with a structure that defines the school of music at Indiana University today. Certainly, this was the vision I embraced when I became Dean.

The curriculum emphasized performance study in private settings and in chamber music coaching. An integral area of study was music theory and literature with historic and stylistic emphasis. There was also a liberal arts component given the setting of a liberal arts institution.

It is important to see how this unique model came about. Herman B Wells was president of Indiana University when, in 1947, he engaged Wilfred Bain as dean of the school of music. Dr. Bain, coming from North Texas State University, wanted to pursue the vision inspired by Dr. Wells.

This vision was to create a comprehensive and self-sufficient school of music in a rather small and isolated town. Performing musicians from the solo and orchestral world would be brought together. Voice, piano, organ, and every orchestral instrument would be taught. The teachers would live in Bloomington and would be joined by permanent academic music professors teaching courses in music theory, history, literature, and composition. Dr. Bain further envisioned that opera was the center of everything needed for a musical experience. To the above-mentioned elements, he added stage design, set design, costume design, and theatrical support. That was the Indiana University School of Music I entered in 1958.

Upon moving to Bloomington, Kenda and I lived in Everman Apartments on campus and spent our days in the few music buildings on campus. We attended private lessons, went to music school classes, practiced, and visited with faculty and students, exchanging ideas during our breaks. Alongside more than one thousand music students and faculty in one central environment, we were virtually consumed by music. This program, unique in the world, was unlike the conservatories or even schools of music generally found in urban areas. There the faculty as well as the students were spread throughout the city with no real chance to exchange ideas or mutual inspiration.

By 1958, quite a faculty had been amassed in Bloomington. I studied with a prominent and distinguished pianist, Walter Robert, who came to the United States as an immigrant fleeing Nazi Germany during World War II. Josef Gingold, Menahem Pressler, Janos Starker, Willi Apel, and Paul Nettl are just a few more persons on a list of prominent performers and scholars at IU, and this list grew rapidly as the student body expanded.

Kenda and I were swept away by everything that surrounded us – the great faculty, the inspiring student body from around the world, the opportunity to study all aspects of music, the advantage of hearing our colleagues making music, and the opportunities inherent in a university setting. We were happily on our way to degree completion.

From the time I entered Indiana University School of Music in 1958, I worked with Dean Bain in some capacity until I became Dean in 1973. I first assisted him as his rehearsal accompanist for the IU Choral Union, which he traditionally conducted. My first faculty appointment came in 1960 as instructor of music and manager of musical organizations. In 1964, I was appointed assistant dean and in 1969 associate dean. At the same time, for four years, I also served the central administration as associate dean of academic affairs. However, I eventually resigned that position because it took too much time from my music activities.

From the beginning, Dean Bain had me work with him in virtually every aspect of the dean's office. Mary Patterson, his first assistant, and I prepared each day's activities beginning every morning with the daily mail and correspondence. He had me prepare routine correspondence for his approval and new and important items for his review and reply. I even assisted with budgetary items, which were carefully guarded in those days. As time permitted, I taught piano, orchestral score reading, and conducting.

As Dean Bain became increasingly busy, I took on more responsibility with the IU Choral Union. My first conducting performance at Indiana University was the *Sea Symphony* of Ralph Vaughan Williams, a huge choral and orchestral piece with soloists and a choir with more than two hundred singers. After this, I prepared and conducted a number of larger choral works in the school of music such as Berlioz's *L'enfance du Christ*, Handel's *Messiah*, and Verdi's *Requiem* as well as full-scale productions of Tchaikovsky's *Nutcracker*, Delibes's *Coppelia*, and Giordano's opera, *Andrea Chenier*. During the 1972–73 season, I conducted the Philharmonic Orchestra with Van Cliburn as piano soloist in two major concertos. During the 1982–83 season, I conducted Douglas Moore's opera, *The Ballad of Baby Doe*, in three performances, and in February 1980 four performances of Gershwin's *Porgy and Bess*.

I.U. choir and orchestra to combine for Vaughan-Williams' 'Sea' symphony

The I.U. School of Music will give its biggest performance of the year when the 200-member Concert Choir combines with the 100-member Philharmonic Orchestra to present Ralph Vaughan-Williams' "Sea" symphony.

The performance will be Tuesday evening at 8 o'clock in the Auditorium with Charles H. Webb Jr., instructor in music and manager of musical organizations, conducting. Soloists will be Bernadine Oliphint, soprano, and Roy Samuelsen, baritone, both graduate students in voice.

Ralph Vaughan-Williams set this, his first symphony, to a text taken from Walt Whitman's "Leaves of Grass." The entire work is highly suggestive of the sea, both in text and music. The four movements are subtitled "A Song of All Seas, All Ships," "On the Beach at Night Alone," "The Waves," and "The Explorers."

Chorus prominent.

The chorus is prominent throughout the work, but there are no separate sections for chorus or orchestra nor any set pieces for the two soloists. All three factors—chorus, orchestra, and solos—are woven into the total composition.

Ralph Vaughan-Williams was perhaps the foremost English composer of the twentieth century; all his compositions are deeply nationalistic. He was on the I.U. campus in October, 1954, four years before his death, and presented his ideas on "The Foundations of Music." He was greeted with a standing ovation.

The combined orchestra and chorus program is an annual event dating back to the early 1920's, when I.U.'s Department of Music was just becoming the School of Music.

Dean Wilfred C. Bain originally planned to conduct this year's concert; however Tuesday he will be attending a meeting in Washington, D.C., as a consultant on music to the United States Information Service. Mr. Webb has been rehearsing the Concert Choir since September, the Philharmonic Orchestra since mid-February and has coached the soloists.

To conduct workshops.

Mr. Webb has been associated with the Fred Waring Music Workshops for the past eight summers as choral conductor, piano soloist, and accompanist.

He has been named head of t workshops this summer and,h appeared as guest conductor choral festivals across the cou try.

Mr. Webb is also a conce pianist. In a duo-piano team wi Wallace Hornibrook, Mr. We has completed five success coast-to-coast tours. Mr. Webb ceived his Bachelor of Arts a Master of Music degrees in t same year, 1955, from Southe Methodist University. He is pi sently completing his Doctor Music degree in piano perfor ance and literature here.

Miss Oliphint is a graduate Texas Southern University a has appeared as guest solo with the Houston and Dallas sy phonies. For two seasons she sa the title role of "Madame Butt fly" in Houston. With the I Opera Theatre this fall she sa Mimi in "La Boheme."

Mr. Samuelsen is a graduate Brigham Young University. just recently completed reco ings of Handel's "Sampson" Salt Lake City with Jan Peer Phyllis Curtin, and Louise Pa er. In 1958 he was runner-up the San Francisco Opera conte and in 1961 he was a regior winner in the Metropolitan Ope contest. With the I.U. Ope Theatre he most recently sa the role of Lazarus in the wor premiere of "The Darkened City

CHARLES H. WEBB

Outside the university, I continued musical activities as a choral conductor, instrumental conductor, piano soloist, and organist. In 1967, I was appointed conductor of the Indianapolis Symphonic Choir, the choral arm of the Indianapolis Symphony Orchestra. During this time, we performed many major choral works including Handel's *Messiah*, Haydn's *Creation*, Mendelssohn's *Elijah*, Bach's *Christmas Oratorio*, and Stravinsky's *Symphony of Psalms*.

At times the conductor of the Indianapolis Symphony Orchestra would conduct the performance, and at times I conducted the chorus and orchestra. It was always a pleasure to conduct this fine orchestra and chorus in major works of choral literature.

In 1978, I prepared the chorus for Berlioz's *Requiem* performances at Carnegie Hall and the Kennedy Center. In May 1987, I was invited to perform an organ recital as part of the Riverside Church Concert Series in New York City.

I was sad when I discovered my conducting activities were cutting into my time as assistant dean, and I felt it was only right to resign and give my full attention to my duties at the music school. While conducting was enjoyable, I could not let it get in the way of my major professional commitment.

Happily, I was able to continue as a pianist, appearing as a soloist with the Indianapolis and Dallas Symphony orchestras. I also continued to tour in duo-piano concerts with Wallace Hornibrook. Our concert tours took us as far away as Australia, where we played a series of fifteen recitals.

Over the years, I also appeared with many IU School of Music faculty artists. Among them were Sylvia McNair, soprano; Josef Gingold, violin; Janos Starker, cello; Margaret Harshaw, soprano; Reri Grist, soprano; James Pellerite, flute; Harvey Phillips, tuba; Patricia Wise, soprano; and many others.

I also made several recordings, including two with James Pellerite on Coronet Records and two with Wallace Hornibrook on the Indiana University Faculty Series and Coronet labels.

The opportunity to make music with artists such as these was an unbelievable learning experience and great inspiration. There could have been no substitute for these contacts on a daily, weekly, or monthly basis.

PART THREE

A Life in Music

CHAPTER SIX

My Continued Association with the Church

MY LIFE AS A CHURCH musician literally began at the age of four and continues to this day. It has been an important part of my life and one I will always cherish.

When Kenda and I arrived in Bloomington, I promptly took on the responsibility at First United Methodist Church as director of the Chancel Choir. During my student days and the time I assisted Dean Bain, I spent two nights per week in rehearsals. One rehearsal was for the church choir and the other the Indianapolis Symphonic Choir. I have fond memories working alongside these excellent singers, some of whom were students at the IU School of Music.

At the church, I sometimes simultaneously played and conducted, but that was the exception. I had fine organists while I conducted and fine conductors when I became organist. David Matthews, a superior player and accompanist, was one of my first organists. Carol Cox, a brilliant player and interpreter of organ literature, served as a remarkable organist for a number of years.

From 1985–1989, I served as an appointed representative on the Hymnal Revision Committee of the United Methodist Church. Organized once per generation, this group discussed the contents of the United Methodist hymnal and made recommendations for deletions and new inclusions. The committee met approximately once per week for several years to bring the current hymnal up to date with practices of congregations and choirs. The committee was also conscious of the quality of tunes and verses and endeavored to include hymns that met a high standard.

Choral conductors with whom I worked at First United Methodist Church Bloomington included my friend, colleague, and administrative assistant Allan Ross as well as Robert Porco, who later became conductor of both the Cincinnati and Cleveland Symphony choruses. I also worked with Jamie Albritten, a very capable student, and Michael Schwarzkopf, a colleague and conductor of the talented Singing Hoosiers.

Now I have the privilege of working with Gwyn Richards, a wonderful friend, colleague, and recently retired Dean of the Indiana University Jacobs School of Music. Dean Richards has transformed the church choir into a superb choral organization, and the singers show their enthusiasm for what he does with excellent attendance and attention.

During my years at First United Methodist Church, many events deserve to be told, but time and space could not begin to accommodate them all. I have chosen a few that stand out.

One notable experience occurred when I asked Josef Gingold if he would consider playing a prelude with me on a Sunday morning. Anyone who knows Joe will know he gladly agreed. He came to me and said he had a very young student who might play the Bach Double Concerto with him. That young violinist was the seven-year-old Joshua Bell! They played to a spellbound congregation, many with tears in their eyes. It was inspiring to see how a talented young boy could draw such emotion from a crowd of two hundred adults.

On another occasion, the church invited a young soprano, Sylvia McNair, to sing. A Metropolitan Opera star, she sang magnificently, her remarkable voice and genial personality making her the love of the whole choir and congregation as well.

In every section of the choir, our soloists came from the school of music and were often heard in major roles on Saturday nights in the IU Opera Theater. These personal experiences were the greatest part of my church music life.

In 1969, I had the privilege of directing the world premiere of Dave Brubeck's cantata *The Light in the Wilderness* at First United Methodist Church. Mr. Brubeck traveled to Bloomington to play the solo piano parts of this exciting new work.

On May 18, 2008, at the fiftieth anniversary celebration of my being organist or choir director at First United Methodist Church, I was asked to give the Sunday sermon. Titled "Celebrating Our Heritage," I include it below in its entirety.

> Today is a first for me, and I'll tell you why in just a moment. It was fifty years ago this year that Kenda and I came to Bloomington for the first time and began worshipping at First United Methodist Church. We heard a magnificent sermon by Benjamin Garrison and never left. So, for fifty years, this has been our church home. Our four sons were baptized here, and Kenda's memorial service was held in this sanctuary.

> During the time I have been a member of this church, I have played for approximately five thousand worship services, I've served on numerous committees, and I've served food in the Wednesday Pantry of the Shalom Center, but I've never preached a sermon. So today is a first for me.

> We are celebrating heritage, and just what exactly is heritage? Webster's defines heritage as "that which is inherited, and also a condition or status into which one is born. The most comprehensive term may imply anything that is passed onto one's heirs or to generations that succeed such as an estate, a tradition, or a right." That's what Webster's tells us.

> Today, we talk about the history and heritage of First United Methodist Church in Bloomington not only to remember our past

and express gratitude for that but to use this distinguished past as a springboard for our future.

Why is it important to do this? It is because of the tremendous debt we owe far-seeing forebears who gave us the rich and vibrant heritage we truly inherited through no effort on our part. We are sitting today in the fifth sanctuary constructed for First United Methodist Church. The land for the first building was given in 1819, only three years after Indiana became a state and one year before Indiana University was founded. There have been more than sixty ministers in this church in its almost two-hundred-year history. As you have already heard, in 1909, the cornerstone for our present church was laid and a beautiful and massive stone structure was dedicated on September 20, 1910. However, on April 7, 1937, a fire broke out under the roof and the church was virtually destroyed. Before the ashes had cooled, a congregational meeting was held in the First Christian Church just one block away, and a unanimous vote of the congregation gave instructions to the trustees to begin rebuilding First Methodist Church.

We have so many things to be thankful for today, but I want to talk about just one for the moment. This is something I know something about, and that is our pipe organ. The church had a pipe organ in 1909. It was a three-manual Estey organ, a middle-of-the-road instrument, but it served the church until it was totally destroyed in the fire. They had to buy a new pipe organ. The church leaders were far-seeing in those days and went to a company in Louisville called Pilcher, where they purchased an instrument several steps above what they'd had before the fire. The pipes we have in the organ today are mostly Pilcher pipes that were added in 1938.

I always give a little talk to the confirmation class before they join the church, and one thing I ask them is, "Do you have any idea how many pipes are in this organ?" Inevitably, one enterprising young person says, "Yes, I know; there are twenty because I count them and they are right up there." Now what they don't know, and what they're surprised to hear, is that behind those pipes are more than three thousand others. Just to give you an idea of what we have and what we owe our forebears in this situation, Indiana University Jacobs School of Music recently signed a contract for a new organ. The organ will be slightly larger than the one we have here but not by much. The cost of the new organ in the school of music is approximately two million dollars. That is what it would take to replace the organ in the church today. It was enhanced in the 1950s when Dr. Oswald Ragatz, the chairman of the organ department, played here. He wanted a fourth division added to the organ, a Positiv division that consisted of ten ranks of pipes from Aeolian-Skinner, which was the Cadillac of American pipe organs in those days. After I came, the console of the Pilcher needed replacing, and we purchased a new console from Moller. They put in new reeds and revoiced the entire organ. So what we have today is a combination of three builders of stops that serve our church in a wonderful way.

On the day of that dedication in 1938, the minister of the church was Dr. C. Howard Taylor, who was also a poet. I think it is very fitting that we hear his poem today:

Above the ashes of our buried past

There rise today the walls and towers of beckoning hopes.

That which has been will be surpassed by that which is to be

That as this temple which we dedicate today

Is ampler than the former house which occupied this spot

So here within these sacred walls

There shall arise a fellowship of faith and hope and love in Jesus Christ

Which will excel all fellowships we hitherto have known.

The artisans in steel and stone and wood

Have finished well their task.

We now begin our work of building living stones into a temple beautiful

Which shall fulfill the earnest of our faith.

I think Dr. Taylor spoke beautifully about the future of this church, and it certainly has been borne out with living stones.

I also want to tell you a brief story that pertains directly to the subject we are talking about today. It concerns one of America's most spectacular actors, Paul Newman. We have all seen him in countless films and perhaps we have eaten some of the food he and a friend started in a small way that grew to be a great business, Newman's Own salad dressings, condiments, and other things. In a biography, Paul Newman says, "I was uncomfortable making money from food and so my friend and I organized a foundation. Every December, with the help of our board of directors, we determine where the profits that have been made from the food we have manufactured will go."

They review many requests, and one particular year, a request came from a Florida school district in southern Florida in the rural part of the state. It had a bus that brought all the children to school. The bus broke down and therefore the children could not get to school. They made an application to the Newman Foundation, which discovered that all the facts were correct, so they presented this school district with a new bus. Paul Newman says in his biography, "The most important letter I got during the entire year came from a six-year-old boy, and it consisted of two sentences: 'Dear Mr. Newman. Thank you for the beautiful bus. Because of you, someday I am going to be somebody. Love Peter.'" Newman says, "That is the most important letter I received because that is all there is to say. There is nothing more."

That story, I think, pertains to each one of us today. We all have people in our past who made this critical difference for us. It might have been a parent, a grandparent, a teacher, a friend, or anyone who touched us deeply and helped to make us "somebody."

When I think of the heritage of this church, I think of people whose vision, integrity, generosity, and perseverance made possible what we have today. I think of people like Herman B Wells, Harry Day, Anna Adams, Lois Ludwig, John Porter, the Hoadley family, Ross Marrs, and many, many others. You should create your own list of people like these whom we have to thank for this great institution that today is First United Methodist Church.

But it is not enough just to remember our heritage. We have an obligation to children, to grandchildren, and to countless numbers of people we never will know. We have an obligation to maintain and enhance our church so that the heritage we leave will be even stronger than the one we inherited.

Let's remember Peter's letter. But now, instead of the name of Paul Newman, put your own name in that sentence. Whom do you have to thank? I think of people like Gloria and Joe Emerson, Gay Hudson, Celicia and Henry Upper, and David Huber. It is also because of people like you that it is possible for this church to continue to provide inspiration, security, strength, and imagination into the future. And truthfully, yes, because of you and countless others like you, we will be strong well into the future.

One year after this sanctuary was dedicated, King George VI gave a Christmas message to all of England that included this brief poem titled "The Gate of the Year":

I said to the man who stood at the Gate of the Year,

"Give me a light that I may tread safely into the unknown."

And he replied, "Go out into the darkness, and put your hand in the Hand of God.

That shall be better than light, and safer than a known way."

That's the best advice we can receive this morning. Let us go forth from this place putting our hands in the hands of God. With His help, our church will remain strong and vibrant for generations to come and we will continually be inspired to celebrate many future Heritage Sundays.

Will you pray with me, please?

Eternal God, as we today tread into the unknown, help us put our trust, our faith, our hands in your hands – hands that are safer than a known way. May we be inspired to leave for those who come after us a stronger, more caring, and more meaningful church so that the heritage we leave will indeed be pleasing in Your sight. In the name of Christ, we pray. Amen.

Someone in the church thought I must surely hold a longevity record. They contacted the headquarters of the Methodist Church in Nashville, Tennessee, to inquire. They were informed that the church did not keep such records, but they knew of someone who had played at the same small Methodist Church in Indiana for seventy-two years. I don't see myself having such an attendance record, but I intend to continue playing at First United Methodist Church as long as the church desires my services.

CHAPTER SEVEN

Home and Family

YOU HAVE ALREADY BEEN INTRODUCED to my wonderful wife, but now I have the pleasure of disclosing additional interesting information. Kenda was born in Amarillo, Texas, on June 18, 1938, and grew up in Big Spring, Texas. She attended SMU in Dallas and transferred to Indiana University School of Music in 1958, where she graduated with a major in music therapy.

She was president of Upper-Webb Interiors for thirty-two years and specialized in interior design for residences, businesses, and professional offices. She also was a member of the Board of Trustees of First United Methodist Church in Bloomington and taught Sunday School for more than twenty years.

In 1997, she received the Sagamore of the Wabash Award, the state's highest award for meritorious service. She is also listed in Who's Who in America and Who's Who in American Women.

In George Logan's history of the Indiana University School of Music, he wrote, "Kenda was one of Dean Webb's greatest strengths in building and maintaining the school of music." Everyone who knew Kenda was touched by her gracious sincerity, kindness, and generosity. As mentioned, at the time of my retirement, she estimated that she had served more than 30,000 meals in our home as first lady of the school of music.

Kenda is the mother of our four sons, Mark, Kent, Malcolm, and Charlie. It is a great pleasure to report that all of them are gainfully employed and living interesting and fulfilled lives. Our oldest, Mark, is an attorney in Indianapolis and a specialist in alcohol-related law. Number two, Kent, is a vascular surgeon and has lived most of his adult life in Tyler, Texas, Malcolm is a financial advisor in Bloomington, and Charlie owns Call Net Call Center, a telephone answering company in Bloomington. We have been blessed with 10 wonderful grandchildren, Tyler, Jimmy, Daniel, Mary Kathryn, Matthew, William, Haiz, Marie Claire, Chase, and Wesley.

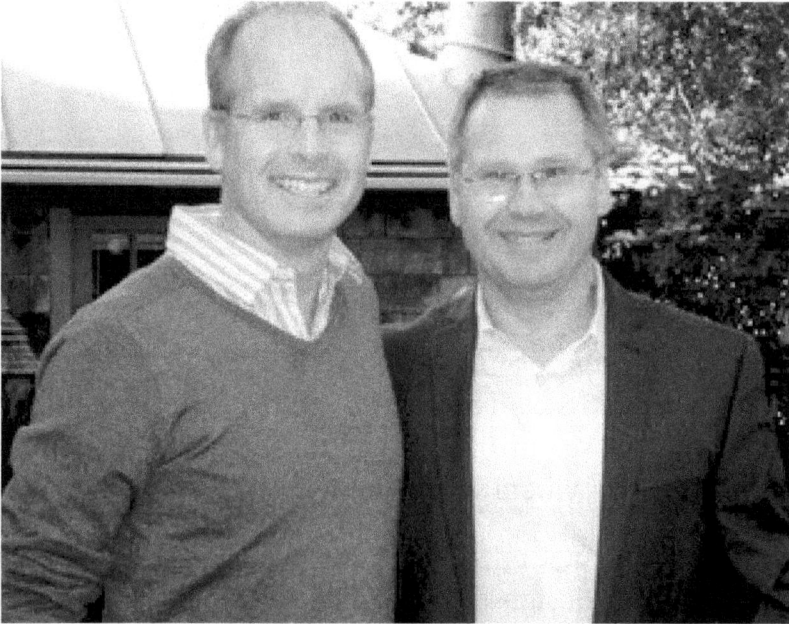

Kent and Charlie in a relaxed setting

Mark in the living room of his aunt, Nancy Webb Poole

Malcolm and Bill Turner, a physician on the faculty of Indiana University School of Medicine until he accepted a position on the University of Texas Southwestern School of Medicine faculty

Charles and Kenda with their four sons

In 1989, Kenda was diagnosed with ovarian cancer, and I felt it was in our best interests that I retire. We had plans to take several trips, and we also wanted some unscheduled time together.

We always enjoyed our January trips to Cancun and welcomed family and friends to these excursions. These enabled my sister, Nancy, and Kenda's sisters, Kay and Karen, to enjoy uninterrupted days together at our favorite watering hole.

Kenda and Charles with their four sons, daughters-in-law,
and precious grandchildren

Kenda's death in 2001 left a gaping hole in our family, in our community, and in her role as First Lady of the Indiana University Jacobs School of Music. We are doing our best to carry on courageously and in the manner that Kenda would want.

About a year before she died, twenty-six members of the Webb family gathered in Bloomington to participate in the Bloomington Foundation Annual Walk for Cancer. We walked to honor Kenda, and Mark's wife, our daughter-in-law Lee Ann Smith, had special shirts made for each person. On the front they said, "Miss Kenda's Team," and on the back, "Never underestimate the power of a stubborn southern belle."

On the cancer walk, we paid particular attention to the construction of a columbarium and labyrinth at First United Methodist Church, two special projects Kenda was interested in that many families had strongly supported. A special plaque commemorating Kenda's help in bringing about these two important additions is located at the entrance of the labyrinth.

Fourth Street entrance to First United Methodist Church

After completing the walk, our immediate family was photographed for our Christmas card in 2000. Front row: Mary Kathryn, Matthew, Daniel, Kenda, Charles, Malcolm, Haiz, Janet. Back row: Kent, Lisa, Mark, Tyler, Lee Ann, Jimmy, Charlie, Chase, Wesley, Lisa.

INDIANA UNIVERSITY
SCHOOL OF MUSIC
Seven Hundred Sixty-Sixth Program of the 2001-02 Season

Kenda Webb Memorial

A Celebration of the Life of Kenda Webb

Musical Arts Center
Monday Afternoon
April First
Four O'Clock

www.music.indiana.edu

Program

Introductory Remarks . . . . Gwyn Richards
Dean, IU School of Music

Remarks . . . . Dr. Joe G. Emerson,
First United Methodist Church
of Bloomington

From *Sonata in F Major, Op. 99* . . . . Johannes Brahms
Adagio affettuoso   (1833-1897)
Janos Starker, *Cello*
Menahem Pressler, *Piano*

From *La Traviata (1853)* . . . . Giuseppe Verdi
Di Provenza   (1813-1901)
Timothy Noble, *Baritone*
Charles Webb, *Piano*

From *Sonata for Clarinet and Piano (1942)* . . . . . . Leonard Bernstein
Andantino — Vivace e leggiero   (1918-1990)
James Campbell, *Clarinet*
Leonard Hokanson, *Piano*

From *Six Elizabethan Songs (1962)* . . . . Dominick Argento
Spring   (born 1927)
Sure on this Shining Night, Op. 13 No. 3 . . . . Samuel Barber
(1910-1981)
From *Motet: Exsultate,*
jubilate, K.165 . . . . Wolfgang Amadeus Mozart
Aria: Alleluia   (1756-1791)
Patricia Wise, *Soprano*
Charles Webb, *Piano*

From *Quintet in A Major, D.667*
(Op. 114), "Die Forelle" . . . . Franz Schubert
Andantino   (1797-1828)
Miriam Fried, *Violin*
Atar Arad, *Viola*
Tsuyoshi Tsutsumi, *Cello*
Larry Hurst, *Double Bass*
Menahem Pressler, *Piano*

Chapter Seven

From *Massa Brevis in B-Flat Major, K.275* Wolfgang Amadeus Mozart
    Kyrie
    Gloria

University Singers
William Jon Gray, Conductor

Kenda Webb
(1938-2001)

Kenda McGibbon Webb was born in Amarillo, Texas on June 18, 1938 and passed away in Bloomington, Indiana, on December 23, 2001. That frame of inescapable dates gives no hint of the rich and fulfilling life of accomplishment, devotion and service that was Kenda's.

After attending Southern Methodist University in Dallas, Kenda graduated from Indiana University with a Bachelor of Arts degree in Music Therapy; she later undertook post-graduate study at the New York School of Interior Design. As the president of Upper-Webb Interiors, Inc., a design firm which she and Celicia Upper founded in 1979, she specialized in interior decor for residences, businesses, hospitals and professional offices. Kenda was active in First United Methodist Church for 43 years, teaching kindergarten Sunday school classes for more than 20 years and serving as a member of the Board of Trustees for many years beginning in 1976. In 1993 she became a leader of the Covenant Disciples Group. She also served Indiana University on a major gifts/special program committee of the Indiana University Foundation and was active in the university's Women's Colloquium from its inception in 1996.

In 1997 Indiana governor Frank O'Bannon named Kenda a Sagamore of the Wabash, the state's highest award for meritorious service. She was also a recipient of the State of Indiana House/Senate Resolution honoring her for a lifetime of service to her community and state. She is listed in the Marquis publications *Who's Who in America* and *Who's Who of American Women.*

As the wife of Charles Webb, Kenda served as the indefatigable hostess for the School of Music during the 24 years of Charles's tenure as dean, and she worked to make the School a family, full of love and con-

On April 1, 2002, A Celebration of the Life of Kenda Webb was held at 4:00 p.m. in the Musical Arts Center. It included introductory remarks by Dean Gwyn Richards, words from Dr. Joe Emerson describing Kenda's career, and a concert featuring some of the most renowned musicians of the twentieth and twenty-first centuries with music by Johannes Brahms, Giuseppi Verdi, Leonard Bernstein, Dominick Argento, Samuel Barber, Wolfgang Amadeus Mozart, and Franz Schubert.

cern for students, staff, faculty and guests. During these busy years she and Charles also found time to raise a family of four sons, Mark, Kent, Malcolm and Charles III; a musical glimpse into the Webb household can be found in the movement of Leonard Bernstein's *Arias and Barcarolles* entitled *Mr. and Mrs. Webb Say Goodnight,* a lively vignette of bedtime at the home while the four boys were growing up.

George Logan, author of *The Indiana University School of Music: A History,* wrote that Kenda was one of Dean Webb's greatest strengths in building and sustaining the School of Music. Her warmth and humanity, and her outgoing nature and compassion, he noted, were tremendous assets in fund-raising and in recruiting world-famous faculty and students to IU. At the time of Charles's retirement in 1997, Kenda estimated that she had served meals to 30,000 people during her years as "first lady" of the School of Music. Peter Jacobi writes that "in her supportive way, Kenda was as instrumental in giving Bloomington's music scene its special character as those who administered or taught or produced or performed throughout the past 35 years or so." It is surely no exaggeration to say that everyone who knew Kenda was touched by her gracious sincerity, kindness and generosity. She frequently remarked that sharing her home with friends and new acquaintances was her way of showing love. A shy, homesick student was as welcome in that home as the most renowned musician.

In her final eight years Kenda fought with great dignity against the cancer that eventually claimed her life. Sustained by her faith and the support of her family and friends, she gave few outward signs of the struggle that the illness demanded of her. It is both profoundly affecting and movingly appropriate that, on the evening she died last December, Kenda was thinking of others: though confined to her bed, she was hosting a party at her home for the nurses who had cared for her during her illness. Our world is diminished by the loss of so remarkable a human being, though we are comforted and sustained by the courage and grace of a life so beautifully and completely lived.

— Compiled by Eugene O'Brien from articles by Doug Wilson,
Peter Jacobi and George Logan

The Herald-Times

WEDNESDAY

DECEMBER 26, 2001 • VOL. 125, NO. 191

4 SECTIONS • BLOOMINGTON, INDIANA • 50¢

Kenda Webb died much as she had lived, at home, surrounded by family and friends

By Doug Wilson
H-T Staff Writer

Kenda Webb frequently said that sharing her home with friends and new acquaintances was her way of showing love.

And few in Bloomington have ever shared their home like Webb. Whether you were a world-famous musician or a shy, homesick college student, you were always welcome at Webb's table because she never tired of having guests.

By her estimate, she entertained 30,000 people at the Woodcrest Drive home she and husband Charles Webb bought in 1967.

On Sunday evening, she invited friends for one last party and died before it ended.

Celicia Upper, one of Webb's best friends, said that having the party though knowing her eight-year battle with ovarian cancer was coming to an end epitomized the 63-year-old's deep concern for others.

▶**INSIDE**
Obituary / A2

Although she was too weak to get out of bed on her own after being released from Bloomington Hospital, Webb and her husband decided to hold a party to thank the nurses who cared for her during her illness.

Barbara Voakes, an oncology nurse who attended, said no patient had ever invited the nurses to his or her home for a party on their behalf.

"That party was the perfect Kenda," said Upper. Webb's part-

▶See WEBB / Back page

Kenda and Charles Webb pose for a photo at a party on Nov. 28. This was one of the last photos taken of Webb before her death. PHOTO BY PAT AH HADDAWI

Kenda McGibbon Webb, 63

JUNE 18, 1938 – DEC. 23, 2001

Kenda McGibbon Webb, 63, of Bloomington, died on Sunday, Dec. 23, at her residence following complications from ovarian cancer. She was president of Upper-Webb Interiors, Inc., an interior design firm that specializes in interior designs and decoration for residences, businesses, hospitals and professional offices, which she founded, along with Celicia Upper, in 1979. She was the wife of Charles H. Webb, dean emeritus of Indiana University School of Music.

Mrs. Webb was born in Amarillo, Texas, on June 18, 1938, the daughter of Kenneth H. and Matilda G. McGibbon. She moved with her family to Big Spring, Texas, where she graduated from Big Spring High School. She attended Southern Methodist University and graduated from Indiana University School of Music in 1961, with a Bachelor of Arts in Music Therapy. She later did post-graduate study at the New York School of Interior Design. From 1961-79 she served as a private music teacher in Bloomington.

Mrs. Webb was active in First United Methodist Church for 43 years, teaching kindergarten Sunday School classes for more than 20 years and serving as a member of the Board of Trustees for many years beginning in 1976. She was a leader of a Covenant Disciple Group in the church from 1993 to the present time. She also served Indiana University on a major gifts/special projects committee of the Indiana University Foundation and was active in the Women's Colloquium since its founding in 1996.

In 1989 she was a recipient, through Upper-Webb Interiors, of first prize in the Bloomington Home Show Competition. In 1997 she received a Sagamore of the Wabash award from Governor Frank O'Bannon, the state's highest award for meritorious service. She was also a recipient of State of Indiana House and Senate Resolutions honoring her for a lifetime of service to her community and state. She is listed in the Marquis publications *Who's Who in America* and *Who's Who of American Women.*

Her memberships include PEO, National Society of Arts and Letters, Friday Musicale, Mortar Board, a lifetime member of the Friends of Music, Mu Phi Epsilon, where she was a founder of the alumni group, and Kappa Kappa Gamma Sorority.

She is survived by her husband and four sons; Kent of Tyler, Texas, and Malcolm and Charles III, both of Bloomington; her mother, Tillie McGibbon of Dallas; two sisters, Kay Werlein of Houston, Texas and Karen Stephenson of Dallas, Texas, and eight grandchildren.

A memorial service will be held at First United Methodist Church of Bloomington on Thursday, Dec. 27 at 11 a.m. Friends may greet the family immediately following the service in the Gathering Space of the church.

A memorial concert will be set at a later date.

Webb died as she had lived

▼**Webb** / from **A1**

ner since 1979 in an interior design firm. "There was so much warmth in that house."

Webb's reputation for throwing parties began after her husband was named dean of the Indiana University School of Music in 1973.

In becoming the school's first lady, Webb worked to make it a family, full of love and concern for students, faculty and guests.

George Logan, author of *The Indiana University School of Music: A History,* said Dean Webb's wife was one of his greatest strengths in building the music school to the world's largest. Her warmth and humanity, he said, was a tremendous asset in recruiting world-famous faculty and students to IU and in fund-raising.

"She's the type of person you genuinely feel privileged to know," Logan said. "I don't know anyone else like her."

When Charles Webb retired in 1997, IU gave Kenda equal billing in holding "A Day of Music and Celebration Honoring Kenda and Charles Webb."

But concern for IU was not the seed for Kenda's kindness. Her love for others grew from her Christian faith.

She taught Sunday school at First United Methodist Church for more than 20 years and was a leader of a covenant disciple group since 1993.

Kirk White, IU special assistant for external affairs and former Monroe County commissioner, remembers Webb sitting with her four sons every Sunday in the balcony at First United Methodist. Charles didn't sit with them because he is the church organist.

Webb would greet everyone who sat in the balcony, especially college students, said White, who met Webb at church as an IU freshman in 1980. The Webbs became the "Bloomington parents" of numerous students, including White, one of many to be considered a "fifth son."

"She always had dinner for as many young people as the boys would have over," White said. "Those are special memories for all of us."

White says many local women, including his wife, Jan, look at Webb as the person after whom they would most like to model their lives.

"Though she's not with us anymore, she's left a legacy in people who aspire to be the kind of person she was," White said.

At Sunday's party, Webb's impact was felt again, though she was no longer conscious.

Early Sunday morning, Webb awoke short of breath. Her son, Kent, a physician, knew the end of his mother's life was near and gave her strong painkillers to make her more comfortable.

She slipped into a coma. Nonetheless, Charles decided to go ahead with the party for the nurses because it was what Kenda would have wanted.

The nurses and their spouses, along with Webb's entire family and several close friends, gathered at the Webb home at 6 p.m.

About 30 people visited Webb's bedroom and spoke to her, although she was still unconscious. They read her favorite Scriptures and listened to her favorite Christmas songs recorded, with Charles playing piano and daughter-in-law Janet Jarriel singing, on CDs that each guest took home.

At 6:45 p.m., while guests ate dinner, Webb passed away.

The nurses decided to stay and wash dishes while family members attended to Webb.

"To be allowed to be a part of that moment was a precious gift," Voakes said. "To the end, she had remarkable dignity and grace. I've never known anything like this."

Reporter Doug Wilson can be reached at 331-4369 or by e-mail at dwilson@heraldt.com.

Peter Jacobi, principal critic for the Bloomington *Herald-Times*, wrote the following statement: "In her supportive way, Kenda was as instrumental in giving Bloomington's music scene its special character as those who administered or performed throughout the past thirty-five years."

Christmas has always been a special time in the Webb family. Beginning with the first Christmas we spent as a married couple in 1958, Kenda and I selected a poem we used as a Christmas greeting to our friends and family. Each year, we spent considerable time perusing dozens of possibilities before coming to a final selection. After Kenda's untimely death in 2001, I continued the same tradition, knowing that would be her wish. After fifty years, I compiled a book that included a copy of every Christmas card we had sent. I still enjoy sending a special poem every Christmas to our family and friends.

During my years as Dean, Kenda and I hosted numerous large parties that featured faculty, administration, and others who were important to the development of the school. On one particular occasion, we invited all the faculty and a number of key supporters to our home for dinner. We probably had more than fifty people on that particular occasion. After a four-course meal and numerous conversations, the guests departed and Kenda and I sat down on the sofa in the living room to relax. Suddenly, she said, "Are you looking at what I'm looking at?"

Upon gazing at the ceiling, I discovered that during the afternoon, our four boys had played a game, not unusual for them, that involved throwing pieces of underwear up over the beams. All Kenda could think of was how many guests might have seen six or eight pairs of underwear draped across the beams.

On another occasion, the cleaning lady of the family next door came to our backyard to inform us that Charlie, who at the time was three years old, was stuffing pebbles into his nose. This required a trip to the pediatrician and involved a lot of screaming by Charlie and a lot of scolding by Kenda. He never did it again.

On another occasion, Kenda looked out of the kitchen window and saw that Charlie was on the roof of the school building next to our property. It turns out that on numerous occasions, his older brothers had talked him into climbing to the roof and jumping into a set of bushes. She couldn't believe her eyes and of course immediately stopped this dangerous behavior.

During a winter season, the boys lost three pairs of gloves and Kenda told them that she'd bought three pairs and that was all she was going to buy. Henceforth, the boys went to school without gloves. One morning it was so cold that they were crying when they arrived at school. One of the secretaries asked why we weren't wearing gloves and they told her their mother wouldn't buy any. A teacher standing nearby offered to purchase gloves, but another faculty member who had overheard the entire incident asked if she knew where the family lived. When the teacher said no, the faculty member pointed to our house and said, "They live right there, and it won't be necessary for you to purchase gloves." Naturally, when Kenda heard this story, she raced to the store and purchased more gloves.

As our family increased in size, we needed additional space as our home on Glenwood Avenue was not large enough. On a cool afternoon in September 1969, I received a telephone call from Ross Robertson, a professor of business economics and public policy who loved music and attended many concerts in the school of music. He told me he had heard Kenda and me speaking about needing additional living space, and he had a great idea. He and his wife had just built a beautiful new two-story house in a rapidly developing area of Bloomington. They wanted us to be their neighbors and he'd found a perfect lot on which we could build our dream home. I told Ross I appreciated his thinking of us but that the area was simply too expensive.

Ross, who would not take no for an answer, had a plan. We should buy the lot, which was just two doors away from his house, and pay on it for one year as if a house were on the lot. He predicted that we would find we could afford to do so. If not, he promised he would buy the lot from us at the full price we'd paid.

Well, that was a win-win situation. We accepted his very generous offer, and at the end of a year we discovered we could carry out Ross's plan. Several months later, we hired the same architect Ross had used, Roll McLaughlin of James Associates of Indianapolis, and built our dream home. It has been a marvelous place to live for fifty years and to rear our family as well as host numerous events for the school of music.

648 Woodscrest Drive,
Kenda's and Charles' residence built in 1969

Swimming pool and gazebo at 648 Woodscrest

Artists' sketch of 648 Woodscrest

One of our favorite additions to the property was a very elaborate tree-house. Kenda had grown up in Big Spring, Texas, with a treehouse in the backyard. Her greatest joy was spending time there with friends and family, and she often talked about her desire to have a treehouse in our back-yard in Bloomington.

During one of our excursions to Europe, our son, Charlie, decided to surprise his mother by building a treehouse while we were away. This was not to be an ordinary structure but one with an architectural plan and a spiral staircase to enter. Charlie designed it to have two levels, both reached by the elaborate staircase.

I never saw anyone as excited and thrilled as Kenda when she laid eyes on that treehouse for the first time. It quickly became our go-to place for lunch every day that weather permitted. You will see the completed activity when the immediate family (eighteen persons in all) gathered for our annual Christmas card photo in December 1999. Unfortunately, as years passed, the two-by-fours that held the treehouse in place were gradually pushed out by growing tree limbs until it was no longer possible to occupy our grand escape. However, we are considering having the treehouse rebuilt so that we can continue to make great memories.

Family Tree House

On two occasions, Kenda and I were invited to be guests at the White House. The first was a celebration of the fortieth anniversary of Vladimir

Horowitz' playing in the United States. Horowitz played a concert in the East Room of the White House and afterwards guests were served a buffet lunch. It was an exciting and wonderful occasion.

To Charles Webb
With best wishes,
Nancy Reagan

To Kenda Webb
With best wishes,
Nancy Reagan

Kenda and Charles greet Nancy Reagan in the White House at a reception after a concert by Vladimir Horowitz

Our second invitation to the White House was put together by Robert Shaw and featured music performed by outstanding student choral groups. One of the performing groups was a choral ensemble from IU, and of course Kenda and I were thrilled to be included in this celebration.

I could write forever about the memories I have of home and family. Suffice it to say I have been abundantly blessed.

The President and Mrs. Reagan
request the pleasure of your company
at a concert and reception to be held at
The White House
on Wednesday afternoon, April 6, 1983
at five o'clock

In this next chapter, I shall try to outline the major responsibilities of a dean of a major school of music. In my judgement, the single most important duty of a dean is to make faculty appointments that enhance the quality of the various teaching components. The dean himself or herself does very little teaching. There is no time to become immersed in the teaching process no matter how interested one might be.

CHAPTER EIGHT

The Dean Years

WHEN I WAS NAMED DEAN of the Indiana University School of Music in 1973, I had the good fortune of having been mentored by Dean Wilfred C. Bain, who had built the faculty to more than 150 members for a student body of 1,600 students.

I shared Dean Bain's basic philosophy of a structure supporting the highest aspects of music training and intended to maintain and build on a teaching faculty that would help students learn and participate in an exciting, combined performance and academic program. The faculty would attract the most promising and talented students from around the world and create a first-class, world-renowned music school. To achieve this goal, I focused on expanding early music and contemporary music programs and was grateful to have the opportunity to appoint outstanding faculty to build both areas.

I also had a plan for improving the school's standing in the world of music and to move it from being nationally recognized to being internationally recognized. This was accomplished by sending soloists and ensembles to perform in world cultural centers and by receiving such performers and teachers in Bloomington. The IU School of Music started this exchange by sending an opera by John Eaton, one of the professors of composition on the IU faculty, for production at the Moscow State Conservatory in the spring of 1990. An agreement was also made to invite the outstanding Russian pianist and teacher Lev Vlasenko to come to Bloomington and give master classes with an emphasis on Russian music. After executing this plan, we became the largest school of music in the nation and were chosen number one in quality by the *Chronicle of Higher Education*, *Change: The Magazine of Higher Learning*, and *U.S. News & World Report*.

Target

Dean Webb outlines U.S.-USSR agreement for music exchange

By Donita Hadley
IU News Bureau

Charles Webb, dean of the Indiana University School of Music, has recently returned from the Soviet Union, where he participated in negotiating the first long-term agreement between the United States and the USSR for cooperation in the education of musicians.

Webb traveled to the Soviet Union in July as one of three U.S. members of the U.S.-USSR Commission on the Education of Musicians. The agreement was signed July 28 in Moscow after negotiations between the U.S.-USSR Commission on the Education of Musicians of the American Council of Learned Societies and the Ministry of Culture of the USSR.

"While in the Soviet Union, this commission finally accomplished something that has never before been done," said Webb. "That is the exchange between U.S. and Soviet music schools and conservatories that will involve among other things master classes, performance of opera productions and music ensembles. To have this agreement signed and approved at the level of the American Council of Learned Societies and the Ministry of Culture of the USSR is indeed a historic occasion."

The commission was created by the International Research and Exchanges Board, the oldest scholarly exchange organization in America that deals with the Soviet Union.

The group represents the American Council of Learned Societies in regard to the USSR and Eastern Europe, and organizes American participation in this commission on music education as well as commissions in other areas.

With the signing of the agreement in Moscow, the group established with the USSR Ministry of Culture a permanent channel for the administration and sponsorship of cooperation between the two governments in the field of professional music training, primarily at the academic level at music schools and conservatories in the two countries.

United States commission members in addition to Webb are Joseph Polisi, president of the Juilliard School and commission co-chairman; and Gary Graffman, artistic director of the Curtis Institute of Music, who was represented in Moscow by Robert Fitzpatrick, dean of Curtis Institute.

The commission will meet at least once every two years to review the U.S.-USSR conservatory relations and to plan new activities, said Webb. The next meeting will be in the United States.

The commission established the following program of collaboration for the academic years 1988-89 and 1989-90. Several of the projects involve the IU School of Music.

● OPERA COLLABORATION — This will involve opera preparation and production. It is expected that the IU School of Music will be responsible for this first step. According to Webb, the IU Opera Theater — including students, conductor and stage director — will travel to the Soviet Union in the spring of 1990 to present an opera in conjunction with Soviet musicians. "Hopefully," said Webb, "we will be able to present this opera production at the conservatories in Moscow, Leningrad and Tbilisi."

● MASTER CLASSES — An agreement was made to exchange specialists who will give master classes in the conservatories of the United States and the USSR. "I'm hoping that in the spring of 1989, Soviet pianist Lev Vlasenko will be able to come to IU and give master classes with an emphasis on Russian music," said Webb.

● MUSICOLOGY — The sides agreed to exchange researchers (advanced graduate students and faculty) for up to two months beginning in the 1989-1990 academic year. Malcolm Brown, chairman of the IU School of Music musicology department, serves on the U.S. commission and will attend a meeting of U.S. and Soviet musicologists scheduled in October at Tufts University in Boston.

● CONCERTS — It was agreed to facilitate the giving of master classes by conductors and performing musicians from each country traveling in the other country on concert tours, including extending their stays for this purpose when appropriate.

● ENSEMBLE EXCHANGE — The negotiators recognized the importance and usefulness of exchange of student ensembles, ranging in size from chamber groups to symphony orchestras.

● MUSIC EDUCATION — A collaborative effort will be made in the classroom study of music theory, history, performance practice and liberal arts for conservatory students, including the use of computer instruction.

ment also includes the long-term exchange of advanced students and faculty; the exchange of conducting faculty for instruction and performance; and the exchange of materials, including recent scholarly publications, recordings, music scores, etc.

"My impression was Soviets were extremely about the agreement exchange, and that worked long and hard come about," Webb said.

U.S – U.S.S.R. music exchange newspaper article

Following is an outline of my responsibilities as Dean of the Indiana University School of Music. Externally, I operated in a designated structure with the deans of all the schools in the university as well as the top administration.

Internally, the administrative structure gave the deans of the various schools ultimate responsibility for appointing faculty and setting budgets and budgetary priorities. I accepted these responsibilities but changed the structure to accommodate more faculty involvement. At that time, all the university was beginning to embrace faculty governance. As an assistant, I sought faculty input into appointments as well as budgetary matters.

As Dean I had an administrative committee comprised of myself, associate and assistant deans, directors of graduate and undergraduate studies, the director of admissions, and a faculty representative. From the beginning of my tenure, I was fortunate to have a superb committee. Members included William Christ, Associate Dean, who had served very well with Dean Bain. Ralph Daniel, appointed director of graduate studies, had been a student at North Texas State University, had attended Harvard as a student of Dr. Apel, and had brought Dr. Apel to Bloomington to the school of music. I appointed Allan Ross as assistant to the Dean and Henry Upper as director of undergraduate studies. John Nagosky became director of admissions. Later, members of my administrative committee included Allen Winold, Jean Sinor, Vernon Kliewer, David Neumeyer, and Gwyn Richards, who became Dean of the Jacobs School of Music in 2001.

Other committees that were key to the administration of the school of music were the performance policy committee, the academic policy committee, and the academic council with departmental representation. There was also the opera casting committee and the opera and ballet committee. These central administrative groups worked well in dealing with various issues facing a complex school within a very big university structure.

All of this was enough to keep a dean busy and unfortunately left no time for teaching. I did, however, find time to perform occasionally with both faculty and students.

The Musical Arts Center

Shortly before I became Dean, the Musical Arts Center was completed, giving the School of Music one of the premier concert and opera venues in the entire United States. It seats 1,460 persons and has superb acoustics for all types of musical performances. Even after thirty years of constant usage, people come from all over the country to marvel at this space, wanting to know details about how we use it, what we would change if we were building it today, and any negative aspects.

The truth is, we would change very little because it satisfies our needs in every way and we are grateful daily for such a structure. The fact that it is regularly compared with the Metropolitan Opera House with respect to stage size, lighting, and sound possibilities is a source of great satisfaction.

From the beginning of my tenure as Dean, one of my goals was to have more students singing major roles in the opera program. I was convinced that by casting mature graduate students in the leading roles instead of faculty members or guests, we would attract excellent singers who wanted and needed experience at that level. This belief turned out to be exactly right and highly advantageous to the school of music.

I was also very enthusiastic about creating the Summer Festival Orchestra, a large ensemble that includes faculty as well as student performers, to enhance the six student orchestras operated by the school during the regular academic year. Students were enormously enthusiastic about the possibility of sitting next to seasoned professionals in rehearsals and concerts, and they found the experience a tremendous learning opportunity.

We also began an artist recording series featuring our best performing faculty and students. The opportunity to listen to professional musicians in rehearsal and at concerts at any time of the day or night developed into another important learning facet of the school. We also created the Early Music Institute with Thomas Binkley as director and the New Music Ensemble with Frederick Fox as director. Visiting conductors from around the world such as Kurt Masur further enhanced our instructional program.

One committee deserves special mention because it had to do with official state department business. In 1981, I was appointed by Colin Powell to a committee to advise the secretary of state on cultural diplomacy. We met several times, and the discussion centered on cultural ties with Arab nations with planned trips to Egypt, London, and a number of Middle East countries.

The committee planned to meet at least once every two years to review U.S. and USSR relationships. At one of these meetings in New York City, we were honored by the presence of Princess Diana, who spoke of her belief in the importance of exchanges that involved people with high-ranking appointments working in special diplomatic relations.

One of our most challenging and satisfying ventures during my tenure as dean was taking an opera to the Metropolitan Opera House in New York City in 1981. The idea to do so came from Professor of Music Education Miriam Gelvin. Dr. Gelvin was interested in all phases of the development of the music school, and in a meeting of faculty and administrators, she brought up the subject, which greatly surprised everyone present. We had been talking about ways to strengthen our national and international activities, so the thought of performing an opera in the most prestigious and largest opera house in the United States became a major talking point.

The more we brainstormed the idea, the higher the excitement grew, and soon someone said, "Let's contact the administration of the Met and see if they would entertain such a thought." Captivated by the possibility of such a venture, I contacted Anthony Bliss, general manager of the

Metropolitan Opera Company. While he didn't say no, he expressed skepticism that a university opera could be performed satisfactorily in such a cavernous space as the Metropolitan's. "Our stage is nearly identical to yours both in size and in electrical and mechanical components," I told him. This seemed to seal the deal.

A number of our faculty had sung leading roles at the Met and were extremely enthusiastic about the project. After being formally invited to perform, we selected a date that was mutually satisfactory and got to work. We had approximately one month to prepare.

One of our first major concerns was selecting an appropriate opera. We knew we weren't going to schedule *Boheme* or *Tosca*. We also knew we were going to be compared with the best in the world, so we wanted to select a piece that would present our effort in the most favorable light.

We had recently done performances of Bohuslav Martinu's *The Greek Passion* with Tim Noble singing the leading role. After copious discussions with the casting committee and others necessary for such a momentous decision, we decided that a performance of *The Greek Passion* would accomplish our goals.

We were told we could begin unloading scenery and costumes at 12:01 a.m. on Sunday, April 26, but that we had to vacate the hall with all our belongings by Monday, April 27, at 12:01 a.m. Our back-stage personnel told me they could handle this, so we assembled all the necessary ingredients and transported everything to New York.

To put it simply, the production at the Met by the Indiana University Opera Theatre was a smash hit. Even thirty-nine years later, no other university has attempted such a feat.

Tim Noble sings the leading role of The Greek Passion on the stage of the Metropolitan Opera House in New York City on April 26, 1981. This began the single most exciting week in the history of the IU School of Music.

In addition to the opera, we brought four other musical performances to New York City that week. On Saturday, April 25, several chamber ensembles from IU performed in Carnegie Recital Hall featuring music of Haydn, Schumann, Barber, and Eugene Bozza. On Monday, April 27, the IU Philharmonic Orchestra played a concert at Avery Fisher Hall at Lincoln Center that included Charles Ives' *Symphony No. 4*. On Thursday, April 30, an IU chamber choir conducted by Robert Porco performed six major choral works featuring music of Britten, Barber, Poulenc, Schoenberg, Petrassi, and our own Bernard Heiden. This performance took place at the Abraham Goodman House and drew an overflow crowd. The fifth IU concert in this banner week featured our New Music Ensemble conducted by Frederic Fox and included twentieth-century composers John Eaton, Juan Orrego-Salas, and Frederick Fox.

THE REPUBLIC

Thursday, October 6, 2011 TheRepublic.com Columbus, Indiana

Music legend to play with philharmonic

By Brian Blair
bblair@therepublic.com

Pianist Charles Webb appreciated the thought when he first heard the idea. But he would have rather played a sour note than agree to David Bowden's suggestion.

Webb, the man who led Indiana University's school of music to a No. 1 national ranking in the 1980s and 1990s, remains a longtime friend to Bowden, Columbus Indiana Philharmonic's music director.

So Webb begrudgingly relented to being billed as "A Living Legend" for Saturday's concert with Bowden's Columbus Indiana Philharmonic.

"I understand his reluctance," said Bowden. "But he is a living legend."

The 78-year-old Webb, a music competition judge, consultant and performer worldwide, agreed that the label that perhaps fits best in his weekend visit to Columbus is simply friend.

Friend to late industrialist J. Irwin Miller and his late philanthropist wife, Xenia, since the late 1950s. Friend to late, local oil executive and arts supporter Richard Johnson — so much so that Webb will be the Johnson Distinguished Guest Artist on Saturday.

Friend to an array of Columbus churches and their top-notch organs he has played in recitals for years.

Friend of the local architectural tour, even, that he touts as often as possible.

"I love to show Columbus off to friends," said Webb. "And I appreciate very much that they are making this a celebration."

He has performed with Bowden and the local ensemble numerous times, playing George Gershwin tunes on the last visit. This time, he will present Ludwig van Beethoven's "Choral Fantasy" from 1808. The composer improvised the piano part during a festival concert and scribbled it down later.

"When Beethoven was writing music, there was no such thing as copy machines or anything to help make separate parts," said Webb. "So, in many instances, pieces were finished maybe 10 minutes before the performance."

See WEBB on Page A5

If you go

WHO: Bloomington pianist Charles Webb, ex-Indiana University music dean, performing with the Columbus Indiana Philharmonic.

WHEN: 7:30 p.m. Saturday.

WHERE: Columbus North High School's Judson Erne Auditorium.

MUSICALLY SPEAKING: With Webb and music director David Bowden at 6:40 p.m.

IN THE PINK: Male musicians will wear pink bow ties to mark October as Breast Cancer Awareness Month. Women will wear pink ribbons. Audience members also will be given lapel ribbons to wear.

TICKETS: Starting at $10 for adults, $9 for seniors and $5 for students. Information: 376-2638, ext. 110, or thecip.org.

CHARLES WEBB

The idea of a university from the Midwest playing a series of five major events in New York City within the space of one week was unheard of, and we were thrilled to be the first to do so. As far as we can determine, this feat has not been equaled since.

This huge undertaking required great generosity from our most loyal supporters and received extensive press coverage. Andrew Porter, principal critic of *The New Yorker* magazine and the most respected and widely read reviewer in the nation, took it upon himself to cover not only the five concerts within one week but also other events in connection with the lavish NY activities. He was always positive when reviewing IU music presentations, and the publicity we received was invaluable.

The IU Foundation was very pleased with the results and said it could not have bought for one million dollars the advertising that came to the university and the school of music from these events. The natural sequence included continuing a New York series. We were able to accomplish this but pared our offerings to one major event per year. None of those spectacular musical offerings would have been possible without the financial support from many individuals, foundations, and corporations interested in cultural development.

Next is an anecdote from an event in the life of a music dean that many of my friends and associates have found quite amusing. I hope that my good friend and colleague Henryk Kowalski will not object to my telling this story.

One day in the early 1980s, Henryk, then a young professor of music in violin and a very accomplished performer, came into my office and told me he was going to Europe for a week to play several concerts. He wanted to know if I would keep his Stradivarius violin while he was out of the country. He felt it would be too risky to travel internationally with this very valuable instrument and intended to take a different one for these concerts. I reminded him that the school of music had locked and insured storage spaces for valuable instruments, but Henryk felt very strongly that he wanted me to personally keep the instrument.

Though I thought the request somewhat unusual, I told him I would put the violin on the top shelf in my closet and that no one would know about it except Kenda; I wouldn't even let our four children know. This arrangement satisfied Henryk.

In the middle of the following week, another one of our violin faculty members, Tadeusz Wroński, came to my office to report a telephone conversation he'd had with Henryk. Henryk had told him he was flying to Indianapolis and had asked Tadeusz to bring the violin to him at the airport. I told Tadeusz that because of the promise I had made to Henryk the previous week, under no circumstances would I permit him to do that. Tadeusz breathed a sigh of relief and confessed that he definitely did not want to be part of this situation.

Everything went smoothly until that Friday morning, when I received a call from John Ryan, the president of Indiana University. He was in Florida attending a meeting of the board of directors of the Indiana University Foundation. One of the directors, a prominent Indianapolis attorney, had very recently been retained by a European client who was attempting to locate a Stradivarius violin being used by one of our music professors. President Ryan wanted to know if I had any idea where it might be because they had reason to believe the violin might be in danger.

I told President Ryan that I not only knew which professor he was referring to but that I knew exactly where the violin was at that very moment.

President Ryan asked me to speak with the attorney, who then asked me to immediately surrender the violin to local law enforcement authorities.

My head spun as I tried to figure out what in the world was going on. I told the president that based on what I knew at the time, I would not voluntarily surrender possession of the violin.

The attorney told me that his client was en route on his private jet to Indianapolis directly from Brussels and that he had already obtained a court order from the Federal District Court in Indianapolis requiring me to surrender the violin. He also told me that the client and a United States marshal were on their way to Bloomington to execute the order.

Upon hearing this, I felt I needed an attorney to advise me. I immediately phoned Cliff Travis, the university counsel, who told me he'd be right over. He arrived a few minutes later and we waited in my office for the federal marshal.

While all of this was going on, I called Kenda to fill her in and asked her not to leave the house unlocked if she went out.

This all occurred on a Friday morning during our weekly administrative committee meeting in my office. The various committee members had been listening with great interest to these discussions. Now, they suggested I go straight home, retrieve the violin, and bring it to my office.

As I did most mornings, I'd walked to school that day. My associate dean, Henry Upper, volunteered to drive me home. When we got there, Henry waited in the car while I went inside to get the violin. I noticed that Kenda's car was not in the driveway and remembered that she'd told me she had a First United Methodist Church Board of Trustees meeting. Since the house was locked, I wasn't worried, but when I went back to my closet to grab the violin, it was missing!

I immediately called the church and spoke with the principal secretary. She told me that Kenda and the rest of the board were in a meeting and that she had strict orders from the senior minister not to disturb them. I told her this was an emergency and that I needed to talk to Kenda immediately.

When Kenda came on the line, I said, "Kenda! The violin is gone!"

She calmly replied, "Well, when you told me it might be in danger, I put it where I thought nobody would be able to find it."

Imagine my shock and surprise when she told me she'd put it in the washing machine because she didn't think anybody would think of looking for it there!

I made a mad dash to the laundry room and thanked God no one had turned the machine on. Ours was a busy household, and the boys were still living at home. I grabbed the violin, which was wrapped in a blanket, and went back outside to Henry Upper, who was patiently waiting in the driveway.

As if things could get any more complicated, we were blocked from pulling out of the driveway by a Bloomington Police Department squad car with its lights flashing. The officer got out of his car and demanded that we identify ourselves. I told him who I was and that I lived here and he said, "Prove it. We ran the plates on this car and it isn't yours." Fortunately, I had my identification with me and was able to convince the officer I lived here so that we were allowed to leave.

After scattering the contents of my wallet all over the driveway in my nervousness, we returned to my office with the violin, arriving a few minutes before the United States marshal. The marshal presented me with a document that appeared to be signed by an Indianapolis federal judge. I showed it to Cliff Travis and said, "What should I do?" Cliff looked at the document and told me it was genuine.

At this point, Cliff pulled the marshal aside and had a brief discussion with him. He then placed a call to President Ryan and spoke with the attorney who had put this series of events into motion. The two of them agreed that the marshal would escort the violin and me to the First National Bank of Bloomington, where it would be placed in a vault. I was designated keeper of the key to the vault until proper ownership was determined.

That was the last time I ever saw this violin, which was ultimately returned to its owner.

Later that night, Henryk appeared at my front door with a bottle of champagne and a box of chocolates. His first words were, "I think I owe you an apology." In my judgement, that was the understatement of the year, but at least the valuable violin was in safekeeping.

Following are quotations from significant music publications that highlight important events at IU School of Music.

INDIANA UNIVERSITY SCHOOL OF MUSIC QUOTES
1984-88

John Ardoin, The Dallas Morning News, 1988:

"In so many ways, the latest version of Mass surpassed the premiere at the inauguration of the Kennedy Center in 1971. The spirit and energy of the young performers left no doubt that Mass remains a vivid, significant musical achievement."

Peter Haley, Albany Times Union, 1988:

"The Indiana University musicians soared high in a lavish, exuberant realization of Bernstein's extravagant theatre piece. The Indiana troupe did their school proud and all deserve an A. This production will probably never be topped."

Lesley Valdes, The Philadelphia Inquirer, 1988:

"The Indiana students, led by Robert Porco, gave the Mass a terrific, tightly meshed performance."

Charles Staff, The Indianapolis News, 1987:

"The Indiana University Music School has given Benjamin Britten's Peter Grimes *the sort of production that enhances the power and beauty of an already powerful and beautiful work... ...the production says just about everything positive that can be said of this great school."*

Andrew Porter, The New Yorker, 1987:

"Bloomington has, in its Musical Arts Center, one of the best-equipped opera houses in the country."

Harold Blumenfeld, Opera, 1985:

"The consummate precision and style of the playing made it difficult to believe that the players were all students. This goes doubly for the cast of young pre-professionals, who performed taxing roles with a technique and style beyond their years."

Andrew Porter, The New Yorker, 1985:

"A test of a music school's liveliness is its students' eagerness--and ability--to play contemporary music. Indiana University's Music School, at Bloomington, passes with high marks on the strength of the two concerts that its New Music Ensemble brought to Symphony Space."

Margaret Campbell, London Times, 1984:

"The overwhelming impression one gets from [School of Music in] Bloomington is its scope in that it is designed to provide students with a basic training related to the demands of professional musical life.... Professors are drawn from the top ranks of international performing artists."

Indiana University School of Music list of
published quotes from 1984-1988

QUOTES

"The Indiana University Opera Theater ... ranks among the best in the country." -- Opera News

"The new Musical Arts Center [is] widely considered, alongside the Metropolitan Opera House, the best equipped opera theater in the country." -- Opera News

"One of opera's most extraordinary and significant ventures is the Opera Theater of Indiana University." -- Opera (London, England)

"The Indiana phenomenon, thanks to resourceful leadership and to an enlightened legislature, remains a prime factor behind the continuing increase in quality and quantity of musical and operatic performance taking place throughout the United States. Its contribution has been incommensurately great." -- Opera (London, England)

"The music faculty at Indiana University in Bloomington is absolutely mind-boggling." -- Beverly Sills

"Serious music in America is being well tended in the Indiana countryside." -- Newsweek

"Indiana University's School of Music and its combined opera house and concert hall, the spacious and admirably equipped Musical Arts Center, constitute one of the country's major musical assests." -- The Village Voice (New York)

"The Bloomington opera house is one of the best in this country." -- The New Yorker

"The reputation of Indiana's School of Music stands high, and that of its Opera Theater especially so. Several times during three events I attended, I had to remind myself that these were student forces, and not a professional group." -- The New Yorker (Nicholas Kenyon)

"We would be far richer artistically in this country if there were more companies like this." -- New York Post

"Maybe the most powerful impression of my life was a visit to the Indiana University School of Music." -- Mstislav Rostropovich (Music Director, National Symphony Orchestra, Washington, D.C.)

"Indiana University's School of Music has an especially distinguished record of achievement in opera." -- New York Times

"The Bloomington opera theater presents things of national importance." -- Financial Times (London)

"A consistently professional standard of which any opera house in the world could be proud." -- Chicago Tribune

List of published testimonials about
Indiana University Opera Theater

As dean, it was also a great privilege to serve on the juries of numerous competitions and hear music performed just about as well as it can be played anywhere. These included the Liszt-Bartok Competition in Hungary, the Busoni Competition in Italy, the Munich Competition in Germany, the Chopin Competition in Warsaw, the Marguerite Long-Jacques Thibaud Competition in Paris, the USA International Harp Competition, the Queen

Elizabeth International Violin Competition in Brussels, and the Carl Flesch Violin Competition in London.

Webb is judge in Warsaw competition

By Edward J. Moss
IU News Bureau

Listening to Chopin played by talented performers is a delight for many pianists, but listening to 127 pianists perform as much as 10 hours a day over a period of three weeks means mixing work with pleasure.

For Charles Webb, dean of the Indiana University School of Music, his work is his pleasure. Webb, a pianist who gives more than 25 concerts a year, was one of 20 judges at the recent Chopin international competition in Warsaw, Poland. Only one other American was on the panel. He is Edward Auer, a member of the IU music faculty and a former winner of the Chopin competition.

Webb was a stranger to Warsaw, but not to judging music contests. He has been a judge in the Liszt-Bartok competition in Hungary; the Busoni contest in Italy; and the Munich, Germany, competition. As one who has successfully competed in similar contests, Webb understood the pressure the young performers were under. He commented in an interview:

"We listened to 185 hours of piano-playing. All of the contestants handled themselves very well. There might have been some brief memory lapses but these were quickly covered up.

"Playing in this kind of competition is more rigorous than playing a professional concert. It takes at least two years of preparation because of the repertoire requirements. The contestants were not permitted to select in advance what they were going to play."

Even a professional performer can have a memory lapse on occasion, Webb said. He explained:

"Everybody has moments when they suddenly find they do not know what notes come next. You do something to get past that and then your memory returns and you go on, hoping no one will notice."

Charles Webb

When he was not busy judging others' performances, Webb was polishing his own selections for an upcoming concert in Indianapolis. He practiced two hours a day during his time in Warsaw, but even the dean of the world's largest school of music has to break away and do other things. Webb walked around Warsaw, visiting the museums and admiring the way the city has been rebuilt since World War II.

Walking comes as naturally to Webb as music. He walks about 4.5 miles a day by making two round-trips from his Bloomington home to his office. He said this gives him a chance to think and plan his activities without interruption.

Although Webb was a stranger to Warsaw, Indiana University is not. Since 1977, IU has had a Polish Studies Center, which works closely with the American Studies Center at Warsaw University. Among other things, the program provides for an exchange of faculty and students at the two universities. It supports both traditional studies and the performing arts. An IU doctoral student is in Warsaw this year studying choral music.

Indiana University and its School of Music are known in both Eastern and Western Europe, Webb pointed out.

"I was very thrilled to talk with people from the Eastern bloc nations as well as those from the West," Webb said. "They all know a lot about our school, our faculty and our students. They also mentioned our opera and orchestra programs. It was really heartwarming to find out how much they know about IU.

"When I visit a foreign city I go to the U.S. embassy and talk to the cultural attaches. Invariably they know about our school and our programs. The attache at the U.S. embassy in Warsaw said, 'IU has the best relationship in a Polish Studies program of any university in the country.'"

While global awareness of the IU School of Music continues, the people at home are given little chance to forget about the school. Webb said last year the school printed programs for nearly 1,000 programs involving vocal, instrumental and dance performances. He added that 98 percent of the performances are presented without any admission charge.

Some of the most fulfilling musicmaking I have ever experienced has come from contestants who have entered a national or international music competition. Nearly all the contestants prepared themselves carefully and displayed their best efforts. On some rare occasions, a contestant would submit an audition tape that had been performed by another person. Readily apparent at first hearing, the juries I served on quickly dismissed such imposters.

On my way to the Busoni Competition around 1985, a transportation delay in my flight to Milan caused me to miss the express train from Milan to Bolsano. Finding myself aboard a nearly deserted local train, I struck up a conversation with the only person in my car, a young man who I was delighted to discover was headed to the same competition.

He introduced himself as Stefano Vicentini, a bassoonist who was part of the orchestra that accompanied the soloists in the competition. I asked him about his plans for music study and he replied, "I want to enroll in a graduate program in the United States, and my teacher suggested I apply to the Indiana University School of Music in Bloomington."

I couldn't believe my ears. With a grin, I reached into my wallet and pulled out a business card, revealing my identity. A few days later, during one of the breaks in the competition, I asked him to play for me. Upon hearing his ability on the bassoon, I knew he would be accepted and encouraged him to apply. Ultimately, he spent a full academic year in postgraduate studies at IU.

On July 29, 1989, Kenda and I had the pleasure of reliving some of these international experiences by hosting an Indiana University Association Alumni Tour to Munich, Salzburg, and Vienna. In addition to seeing some of the world's most important sights, we took advantage of being in major music capitals of the world. Having led cultural tours in the past, we can easily say that the alumni who participated in this particular tour saw and heard some of the twentieth century's most exciting ventures.

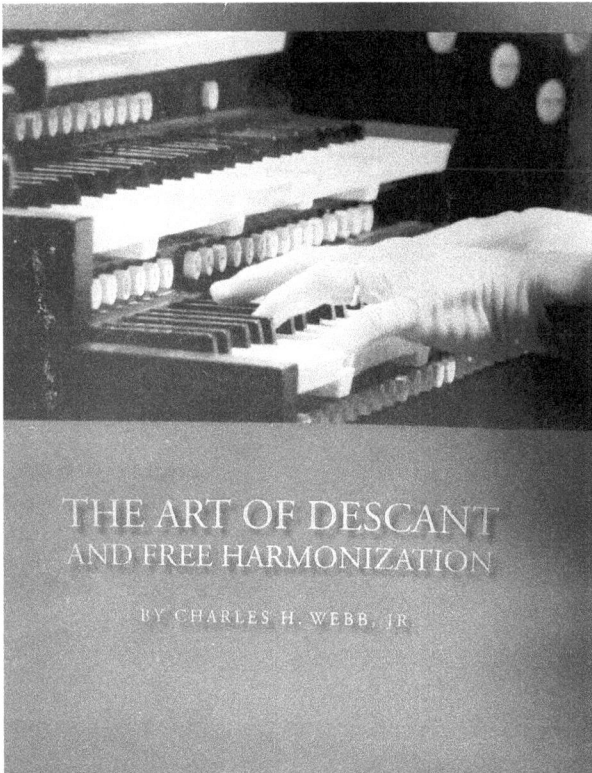

In 1997, I received a Rockefeller Study Grant to go to Bellagio, Italy, for one month for the purpose of writing The Art of Descant. The book was published in 2013 by Indiana University Press.

Being Dean of one of the most prestigious schools in the world was one of the greatest honors and pleasures of my life. Certainly, there were lots of challenges, but they were always outweighed by the joys.

PART FOUR

Looking Back

PART FOUR

CHAPTER NINE

A Fortuitous Bond with Two Special People

MANY PEOPLE ASK ME WHAT retirement is like and if I miss all the meetings and decisions I used to make every day. The truth is, I do not miss those types of things. What I do miss are my colleagues, our daily chats, my regular contacts, and keeping up with their families and friends.

I often said that the world would have to judge the quality of my professional accomplishments but that I would be the best ex-dean around. This meant that, after retiring, I was hands off. I was always glad to help if someone felt my help was needed, but I never offered unsolicited advice to the new dean. I believe I have kept that promise, and I am pleased to say I have heard nothing to the contrary on the subject.

One of the greatest satisfactions of retirement is the ability to participate in activities that are scintillating and interesting but could not be worked into the demanding schedule of dean. I have had many opportunities to attend concerts and lectures that there was no time for prior to official retirement. There has also been more time to practice and perform, both solo concerts and ensemble experiences. I have especially enjoyed more frequent discussions with faculty and friends that sometimes veer from music to politics.

Playing with colleagues in various musical concerts is one of the greatest pleasures I can imagine. For instance, in April of 2001, I played the solo piano part in Gershwin's *Rhapsody in Blue* with the Bloomington Pops Orchestra. Peter Jacobi gave the concert a compelling review, which I am pleased to quote in its entirety below.

More than anything, Saturday evening's "Gershwin Celebration," as realized by the Bloomington Pops at the Indiana University Auditorium, served to remind us how wide and lasting a swath George Gershwin cut across our musical landscape: be it the realm classical in nature, Broadway, film, or Tin Pan Alley. The Pops program included favorites from among all the styles and backgrounds and was the richer for it. But the concert also proved how well the Pops plays Gershwin, particularly if the chosen arrangements help out rather than get in the way. On occasion, music director Robert Stoll selects versions that get fussy or hide primary themes and rhythms beneath a layer of refinements that refines the flavor of the song right out. On the other hand, when he and his players stick to the basics, things work just fine.

D4 • The Herald-Times, Tuesday, April 10, 2001   **LIFESTYLE**

MUSIC REVIEW: 'GERSHWIN CELEBRATION'

Charles Webb the star of Pops' tribute to Gershwin

By Peter Jacobi
H-T Reviewer

More than anything, Saturday evening's "Gershwin Celebration," as realized by the Bloomington Pops at the Indiana University Auditorium, served to remind us how wide and lasting a swath George Gershwin cut across our musical landscape: be the realm classical in nature, Broadway, film, or Tin Pan Alley. The Pops program included favorites from among all the styles and backgrounds and was the richer for it.

But the concert also proved how well the Pops plays Gershwin, particularly if the chosen arrangements help out rather than get in the way. On occasion, music director Robert Stoll selects versions that get fussy or hide primary themes and rhythms beneath a layer of refinements that refines the flavor of the song right out.

On the other hand, when he and his players stick to the basics, things work just fine. All was just right, for instance, during a performance of "They Can't Take That Away from Me." With trombonist David Pavolka around to solo in planned down-to-earth, rough and dirty form, the song came deliciously to life. As did "Walking the Dog," with clarinetist Scott Schleuter tooting ever so freely through Gershwin territory. And concertmaster Juli Enzinger honored "Someone To Watch Over Me" with her sweet fiddling. "Love Walked In," for sure, when Richard Seraphinoff and horn so smoothly told us so. In each case, the orchestra completed the musical picture, and no overly complicated arrangements got in the way.

What stole the nicely played show, however, was the classical Gershwin, thanks to guest soloist Charles Webb, who demonstrated a total at-oneness with the composer, first in the three 1927 Preludes to Piano. The outer ones were solved, for all their rhythmic and embroidered trickeries. The middle one was suffused with the sultriness that, when interpreted correctly, makes its melody the object of wide public favor.

Webb followed up with a facile and irresistibly lyrical interpretation of the *Rhapsody in Blue*, the 1924 Gershwin creation that remains at the top of the composer's classical hit parade. Balances, as is usual with the *Rhapsody*, were out of kilter in various spots due to scoring, but on the whole, Stoll and the Pops gave Webb a supportive collaboration.

The pianist was the star of this performance and of the whole evening. Webb's mastery of the keyboard and his superbly honed musicianship won top honors, hands down. An instantaneous standing ovation was his reward, and a well deserved one.

All was just right, for instance, during a performance of "They Can't Take That Away from Me." With trombonist David Pavolka around to solo in planned down-to-earth, rough and dirty form, the song came deliciously to life. As did "Walking the Dog," with clarinetist Scott Schleuter tooting ever so freely through Gershwin territory. And concertmaster Juli Enzinger honored "Someone to Watch over Me" with her sweet fiddling. "Love Walked In," for sure, when Richard Seraphinoff and horn so smoothly told us so. In each case, the orchestra completed the musical picture, and no overly complicated arrangements got in the way. What stole the nicely played show, however, was the classical Gershwin, thanks to guest soloist Charles Webb, who demonstrated a total at-oneness with the composer, first in the three 1927 preludes to piano. The outer ones were solved, for all their rhythmic and embroidered trickeries. The middle one was suffused with the sultriness that, when interpreted correctly, makes its melody the object of wide public favor. Webb followed up with a facile and irresistibly lyrical interpretation of the *Rhapsody in Blue*, the 1924 Gershwin creation that remains at the top of the composer's classical hit parade. Balances, as is usual with the *Rhapsody*, were out of kilter in various spots due to scoring, but on the whole, Stoll and the Pops gave Webb a supportive collaboration. The pianist was the star of this performance` and of the whole evening. Webb's mastery of the keyboard and his superbly honed musicianship won top honors, hands down. An instantaneous standing ovation was his reward, and a well-deserved one.

Press Release of Senator Lugar

Hoosier Named to National Advisory Committee

Secretary of State Colin Powell accepts Lugar recommendation

Tuesday, March 2, 2004

U.S. Sen. Dick Lugar today announced that Secretary of State Colin Powell appointed former Indiana University School of Music Dean, Charles Webb, to the Department of State Advisory Committee on Cultural Diplomacy.

The new advisory committee is tasked with preparing a report for the State Department and Congress by September 2005. The seven-member committee will prepare recommendations on programs to increase "the presentation abroad of the finest of the creative, visual, and performing arts of the United States," and "strategies for increasing public-private partnerships to sponsor cultural exchange programs that promote the national interest of the United States."

"Dr. Webb will be participating in a critical component of American public diplomacy," Lugar said. "As Chairman of the Senate Foreign Relations Committee, I understand the importance of the United States doing a better job communicating our values to the world, as well as promoting and understanding our mutual interests and cultural diversity.

"We must clearly and honestly explain the views of the United States, displaying the humanity and generosity our people, underscoring commonality, and expanding opportunities for interaction between Americans and foreign peoples," Lugar explained. "Indiana colleges and universities have long been on the forefront of international exchanges and education programs. Dr. Webb's unique insight will be invaluable as we seek to expand and enhance international understanding."

###

218591

Press Release of Senator Lugar

Retirement also afforded me the time to appropriately reflect on the relationships I developed with two uniquely special people who impacted my life personally as well as IU's school of music.

The most generous family to embrace Indiana University in its two hundred-year history is the David H. Jacobs family of Cleveland, Ohio. Mr. and Mrs. Jacobs were both graduates of IU, and they developed a remarkable interest in the school of music following the lead of their oldest son, David Jr. His association with the school is fascinating.

David Jr. enrolled in the freshman class of IU in the fall of 1972 with the intent of majoring in music, specifically organ performance. He began singing in the choir of First Methodist Church shortly after he enrolled. We met him at church, and Kenda invited him to have Sunday lunch with us. He came and never left. He seemed to enjoy hanging out with a family that played together, laughed together, and had fun together. He also served as babysitter on numerous occasions.

On one occasion when he was visiting, he heard me say we wanted to include Beethoven's "Marche Solonelle" in an upcoming orchestra concert but that our librarian had told me the score was unavailable. He said, "Did you say the Cleveland Orchestra performed that work?" When I told him yes, he immediately responded, "Don't worry; my mother will get it for you."

When I expressed my surprise that she could find the score when our librarian could not, he told me that his mother was on the board of the Cleveland Orchestra and that she would mail the music. In two days, by special delivery, the score and parts arrived. That was the first indication I had that we were dealing with an unusual situation.

The second indication came when David told us his parents were coming the next weekend for Parents' Weekend. I asked him if they were going to drive, and he told me that they would be coming by air. When I told him that Bloomington did not have air service, he said they would arrive in their private jet with two pilots. Not the most usual circumstance for students in the school of music!

After a year in the organ curriculum, David came to the conclusion that he could not accommodate the specific requirements of the degree. In considering other alternatives, he had decided he would like to major in English. He'd heard me talk a number of times about my interest in English as a degree subject and the courses I'd taken at SMU as an undergraduate in that field. He applied, was accepted, and transferred to SMU in Dallas to continue his studies, where he enjoyed his coursework and graduated in 1970 with a bachelor's degree.

Throughout his Dallas days, we kept in contact, and Kenda and I were pleased that he was extremely successful in that major. Upon graduation, he went immediately to California, where he began a career in real estate, a field that had interested him his whole life. However, he remained in contact with the IU School of Music, and when his father died, we took special music to Cleveland to celebrate his father's life.

In 2002, David's mother asked him what he would like for his birthday that year. He surprised her with his request. "Mother," he said, "I would like for the IU School of Music to be named for my father." Barbara Jacobs was shocked. "Do you have any idea what that would cost?" she asked.

Soon I received a phone call from David asking how much it would cost to name the Indiana University School of Music after his father. I had no idea, but I knew who would: the president of the university. I soon received a call from President Myles Brand telling me the price would be thirty-five million dollars. When I relayed this figure to David, his response was, "That doesn't sound too bad."

Numerous discussions followed. Sure enough, during the Christmas season of 2002, Barbara Jacobs made a gift bringing the family's total contribution to 42.5 million dollars over a thirty-five-year period. This generosity enabled IU to maintain its number-one position in quality out of more than six hundred accredited schools of music in colleges and universities in the United States and inspired IU to rename the school of music as the Indiana University Jacobs School of Music.

David Jacobs Jr. has been one of the School of Music's most important alumni. Not only has he maintained his strong interest in music and acted as the stimulus to his mother's forty-two-million-dollar gift, but he is also a member of the Indiana University Dean's Advisory Council and has built several homes within walking distance of the music school to support visiting faculty who are in residence in Bloomington for various lengths of time.

Upon receiving the school's Distinguished Alumni Award, David was asked to speak to the entire group assembled. Following is his reflection.

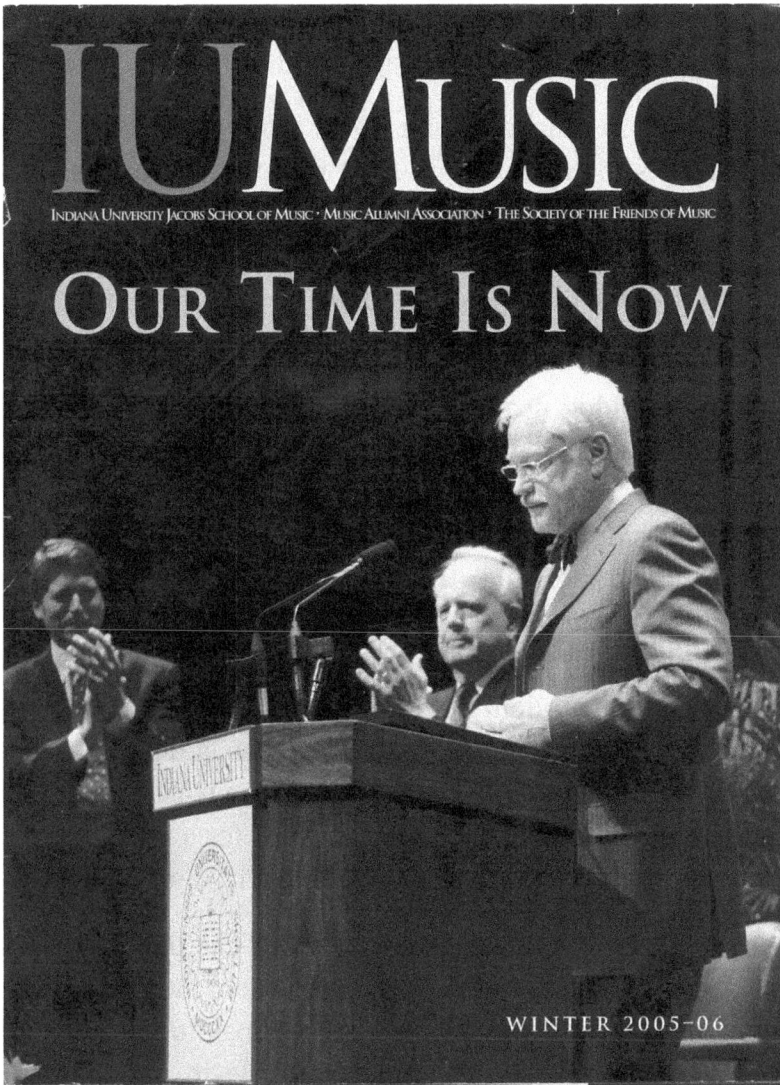

Cover of IU's Music Magazine featuring a speech by David Jacobs,
applauded by Dean Richards and Charles Webb

Good evening and thank you. To begin, I'd like everyone to take a minute and mentally stretch...Take a deep breath...After all, this evening is about celebrating the stretching of our boundaries, my own included.

It's an honor to be a part of tonight's celebration of this truly superlative university and to collectively and collaboratively kick off our bicentennial campaign. And not incidentally, it means a great deal to me personally for this evening to begin with a performance by one of our students from the Jacobs School of Music,

William Ronning. A big round of applause, please, for William... Thank you, William; you did us all proud.

I'm always so touched when I hear from the diverse and talented students to emerge from IU. I'm reminded of the value of education, a gift that brings us all closer to the fullest realization of our potential. So I'll share with you a bit of news this evening, but first, as Pat said, I was a student in the IU School of Music more than forty years ago.

As I grow older – and I am slightly Jurassic these days – it becomes clear to me that the relationships I made while at Indiana University were not only important but had a seminal impact on my life. I have realized that IU was a very special place then and it continues so today, as it is one of the most comprehensive, impressive, and affordable universities in the country. It is unparalleled in its level of dedication – all eight campuses with their 115,000 students. With such recognition, it was also at the IU School of Music that I learned I seriously needed to change my major. Yes, the truth is, being one of the least capable music students then, I dropped out, went to work for a year, and transferred to Southern Methodist, graduating with an English degree.

Now some might find it ironic that for the past five decades I've nurtured my passionate loyalty to a school I voluntarily chose to leave, yet it has always made perfect sense to me because my time at IU was probably the most valuable in my life. This is because of the wisdom, the patience, and the vision of one couple: a man whose singular vision continued and expanded, exponentially, the IU School of Music's remarkable traditions, one of Indiana's Living Legends, Dean Charles Webb, and his openhearted and embracing wife, Kenda McGibbon Webb.

The Indiana Historical Society's
Living Legends Gala 2004

Presented by
American United Life Insurance Company

Five New Living Legends of the State of Indiana

In addition to counting Dean Webb as one of my earliest mentors, I became very close to Charles and Kenda Webb as well as their four sons. The word "genius" is tossed around frequently, but Charles was an administrative genius and remains today one of the greatest collaborative musicians. He demonstrated this miraculous talent of working with tens of thousands of students and hundreds of faculty in his twenty-four years at the school's helm.

Moreover, he helped each of these individuals stretch to realize their fullest potential. He and Kenda exhibited what can only be described as "grace-filled energy." While his capacity of working with young students and giving "space" to a romantic ensemble of faculty can never be minimized, he was also an absolute master at building a music school worthy of legend. He excelled in this collaboration. He selected the most talented faculty (the number one task of any dean since faculty attracts quality students), and Kenda made them all, yes, all, welcome and appreciated. These working professionals – instrumental divas, opera stars, musicologists, musicians in every genre – stretched their own boundaries and came to Bloomington to share their talents and their real-world knowledge with the students who chose to study with this hand-selected faculty in a place surrounded by corn fields.

Even the incomparable Leonard Bernstein, in a dark period of his compositional career, was persuaded by Charles to come to Bloomington to rejuvenate. In the energy of the Webb family, the great maestro rediscovered his mojo and went on to compose an opera to be performed by IU students at the Metropolitan Opera House, part of the Lincoln Center for the Performing Arts. No small potatoes from a field of corn, eh?

I could go on and on about the Webbs, but one thing I've observed over the decades is that Charles' method of teaching, of encouraging, of administrating, of collaborating across all areas is a pure definition of the Indiana University way of doing business.

This is truly about gratitude.

I am eternally grateful that my parents (both graduates of IU) realized through the value of my relationship with this remarkable man, his wife, and family a greater value of Indiana University. In that recognition, toward the end of my mother's life on Earth, she endowed the Jacobs School of Music. The truth is, I explained to her over a Scotch and soda a choice: buy the then-president of the United States another bomb or use the money in an eternally dynamic way to create a lasting explosion, as it were, educating generations.

Believe me, it was to my delight that she did not choose the military bomb option! With that, one of my biggest gratitudes is that I've been able to build on that support and the gifts my parents began decades ago.

Now, some of you may not know this, but my parents were also very comfortable in the world of baseball. Through this world, I learned over time that a winning team is about more than raw talent. Of course that talent must be found and nurtured, but every year it's a new season and every year that same level of finding, building, and sustaining greatness must be continued.

Friends, it is my understanding that humanity is light in its purest form. Reduced to nano-particularity, below our molecular level, where eminent physicists suggest it's "turtles all the way down," when all is said and done, we are but a wavelength. Radiance. What else is music but ordered wavelength?

In harmony and disharmony, music has timber and pitch and rhythm and the power to move people, to lift their souls to a higher dimension. "Drummers beating a tiny time," to quote Wallace Stevens, which we did, and we sang before language was codified.

For two hundred years, Indiana University has performed a majestic, magnificent symphony of promise with understanding, inclusion, accomplishment, thoughtfulness, and wisdom.

As I mentioned earlier, I have been asked to share with you a bit of news this evening of a conversation that began more than a year ago, a conversation that developed out of a relationship I've come to treasure. Tonight, I share with you that I will be making an additional investment of twenty million dollars to the IU Jacobs School of Music. I'm aware that although this gift might seem large, I'm only a small part of a much bigger opportunity. I cannot do this alone. I need you, every last one of you in the audience this evening.

Friends, I am inspired. I am inspired by the current dean of the Jacobs School, Gwyn Richards, whose thoughtful, care-filled, and collaborative approach and molder of our mission's vision continues and expands upon Charles' tradition towards our second century. I am inspired and gobsmacked that we teach more than eighty foreign languages at Indiana University - more than any other university in the world, I believe - as with that communication skillset comes understanding.

I'm inspired to stretch my capabilities. The collaborative relationships I've made at IU represent an awesome power. They inspire me to look inwardly and outwardly, to challenge myself, to think of and develop the necessary questions that shape our world. I realized, through the eyes of a loyal, strong, and kind-hearted man and his grace-filled wife, that I too was worthy of investment. We all are, in our own delicious diversity. Now is our opportunity, our time, to educate and inspire the next chapter of philanthropists through the mission and vision of this enterprise we hold dear. Together, we are charged with the task of propelling Indiana University into its next two hundred years with strength and momentum.

In collaboration, we are capable of so much more than we know, so I ask you to join me, like many are doing - Mickey Maurer, Bob McKinney, Lowell Baier, Jim Hodge, Cindy Simon Skjodt, Pat Miller, Yatish Joshi, Gail and Bill Cook, Nancy and Bill Hunt, and Indiana's great state benefactor in the Lilly Endowment to name a few (though there are many others) - in whatever way you can - and invest in Indiana University. Together we will forecast the brightest future imaginable for IU with all its promise, understanding, inclusion, and wisdom.

Our combined investment will foster and develop such awesome potential. Of course there's an expense, but as Kelly Clarkson sings, "What doesn't kill you makes you stronger," and what value there is in the outcomes!

Together we are a master orchestration, my friends, and I encourage you to sing out and play your finest notes. Whether your passion is in music, the arts, the political science of culture and humanities, applied or theoretical science, business, medicine, or law, please join me in sustaining this magnificent composition, yes, its master orchestration, long beyond Indiana University's next two hundred years.

Another special individual I had the pleasure of meeting through my work at IU was none other than Leonard Bernstein. In 1976, I received a call from Harry Kraut, the general manager of Leonard Bernstein's enterprises, to talk about the opera program at Indiana University School of Music. Mr. Bernstein had been asked by the Israel Philharmonic Orchestra to celebrate the thirtieth anniversary of his first occasion conducting that orchestra, and he decided to do so with a production of his opera *Trouble in Tahiti*. However, he wanted the opera produced with singers approximating the ages of the characters in the opera rather than with seasoned opera stars. He did not know where to find such singers, but he knew about the extensive opera productions in Bloomington and wondered if we might want to undertake such a venture.

It sounded to me like a wonderful opportunity to extend the reputation of our school and opera department. The one caveat was that the opera had to be produced first in Bloomington and viewed by a committee before a final decision would be made. I agreed to those stipulations, and the group that came to Bloomington for judgment was enthusiastic about our production. Soon after, we assembled the soloists, chorus, orchestra, scenery, costumes, and everything required to make the trip to Israel, with all costs borne by the Israel Philharmonic. The students who participated in this exciting venture were ecstatic about the experience and possible future contacts with Bernstein.

Charles greets Leonard Bernstein after
a concert of his music

Best-ever Bernstein 'Mass' performance

By Peter Haley
Special to The Times Union

LENOX, Mass. — The Boston Symphony Orchestra's 70th birthday bash for American composer Leonard Bernstein at the Tanglewood Festival continued on Saturday, featuring a production of his "Mass" by the Opera Theatre of the Indiana University School of Music.

In the composer's own words at the concert's end, "one of the best performances ever, anywhere," the extravaganza was a celebration of the "miracle of youth, faith, America, and Tanglewood."

Using the text of the Roman Catholic liturgy as a framework upon which to hang additional words of social commentary written in the late 1960s, the composer, assisted by Stephen Schwartz, created an appealing libretto.

Written in 1971 at the request of Jacqueline Kennedy for the opening of the John F. Kennedy Center for the Performing Arts in Washington, D.C., "Mass" caused a stir, with its controversial commentary on contemporary religious thought. A blues singer croons, "If you ask me to love you on a bed of spice, Now that would be nice, once or twice, But don't look for sacraments or sacrifice, they're not worth the price," while the Celebrant berates the "congregation" for "Praying and pouting, Braying and shouting litanies, Chanting epistles, Bouncing your missals on your knees."

If that doesn't get the blood pumping, how about "Come love, come lust, It's so easy if you just don't care," or (addressing Jesus) "You said you'd come again, so you made us all suffer, So when's your next appearance on the scene?"

Bernstein and Schwartz clearly set out to jab a lot of sacred cows, and succeeded. "God Said," one of "Mass"'s hit songs, quotes the biblical creation passage and packs a powerful punch as the preacher, in dialogue with his flock, teaches, "God said that sex should repulse, Unless it leads to results, And so we crowd the world, Full of consenting adults," and all respond heartily, "And it was good brother, GODDAM GOOD!"

That Bernstein got away with comments like these, that they flew at all, is attributable to his unique musical genius, which allows him to say exactly what he chooses. (Martin Scorsese, eat your heart out.)

The Indiana University Musicians soared high in a lavish, exuberant realization of Bernstein's extravagant theatre-piece. While the composer's treatment of the liturgical text holds up well, some of the pop-rock passages are thin and wordy, and show wear under the test of time, saved only

SONG — Singers of the Opera Theatre of the Indiana University School of Music perform "Mass" at Tanglewood Saturday to honor Leonard Bernstein's 70th birthday.

by the volcanic energy of the vivacious young performers. Baritone Douglas Webster was totally convincing as the Celebrant, meeting Bernstein's vocal demands — even the consistently high *tessitura* — impressively. Conductor Robert Porco and stage director Jack Eddleman have brought the very best out of the willing students.

The orchestra and two complementary on-stage rock groups play beautifully; both the adult and children's choruses are shining examples of stage deportment,

while the singing actors would be the envy of many a Broadway troupe. The costuming and choreography for the eight acolytes deserves praise, as do the dancers for their gracefull support.

Almost every major composer has been drawn to the inherent drama of the Roman Catholic liturgical text,

The Indiana troupe did their school proud and all deserve an A. This production will probably never be topped.

Several years after that experience, I had another call from Mr. Kraut proposing a new association with Mr. Bernstein. In the process of composing a new opera, Bernstein wanted to be in contact with our opera singers. He hoped they would be willing to sing the roles while he composed new material. They would then sing the new material to Bernstein while he examined various aspects of the composition. If successful, this collaboration would inspire the maestro to continue his work and of course would be invaluable for the singers themselves.

During the two months that Bernstein and his staff were in residence in Bloomington, Kenda and I had ample opportunities to host them in our home. One evening they came for dinner and brought with them a manuscript that began, "Blessed are the Webbs." It was a chorale, and Kenda immediately said, "Mr. Bernstein, won't you please play it for us?" He went to the piano, played it through, and then said to Stephen Wadsworth, his librettist, "Stephen, I like this. I think we should put it in the opera." Naturally, he changed the words to be part of his opera, but the music remains a part of the opera as well as a hymn to the Webb family.

On that same evening, our son Mark and his high school jazz band had scheduled a rehearsal in our basement. We had no idea that Leonard Bernstein would have the tiniest interest in such a thing, but very soon after the boys began playing, the maestro was moving his arms to the rhythm of the music. To our amazement, he climbed upon the Steinway grand piano in our living room, lay face down on the top of the piano, reached beyond the music rack to the keyboard, and began playing part of what the band was rehearsing. Malcolm caught this incident on tape, and we have included a picture of LB (as he liked to be called) in an extremely unlikely position – playing upside down.

Leonard Bernstein

In 1988, a package addressed to me arrived in the mail, and I was shocked when I opened the beautifully gift-wrapped box. In it was a piece of music entitled "Mr. and Mrs. Webb Say Good Night." The words included Kenda's and my names, Mark's and Malcolm's names, and the story of a family considering a move to Chicago. All the words as well as the music were written by Bernstein, and he included this song in a large-scale choral work with orchestra and soloists entitled *Arias and Barcarolles*. It has since been performed all over the world and recorded by numerous major symphony orchestras. Needless to say, we were deeply honored to be remembered in such a fantastic way.

The year 1988 also marked Leonard Bernstein's seventieth birthday. One of the musical organizations that wanted to commemorate this important event was Tanglewood, an institution Bernstein had been closely connected with for many years. When they asked him what piece he would like to hear, he replied that he would like Tanglewood to present his *Mass*. This presented a real problem because Tanglewood did not have the musical forces to perform this huge work.

Bernstein suggested Tanglewood contact Indiana University School of Music and ask them to produce the work. I remember Harry Kraut's telephone call and how excited I was to receive this invitation. We changed our last opera of the season to produce *Mass* in Bloomington before transporting it to Tanglewood.

The entire production of 250 persons included the orchestra, chorus, dancers, children's choir, rock band, and singing and dancing street people. We were told that ten thousand people witnessed this production, and the critics praised our rendition. The audience was extremely enthusiastic, and Bernstein said it was one of the finest things he had ever witnessed.

Without question, my relationship with Leonard Bernstein was invaluable to the IU School of Music as well as to the Webb family.

I also want to emphasize once more the importance of my faculty and staff colleagues in developing and maintaining an outstanding school of music. None of our various accomplishments could have ever taken place without the care, feeding, and never-ending interest of such devoted individuals. We are all fortunate indeed to have lived in an environment that captured such talent and generosity.

Individuals, corporations, and foundations have all contributed to the ongoing strength of the Indiana University Jacobs School of Music. Although the basic underlying financial support comes from the state of Indiana, the interest and contributions of many other entities have enabled us to maintain our position as the premier school of music over a protracted period of time. We pledge to all those contributing entities, and to those who come in the future, our undying efforts to maintain the strongest possible school long into the future. What a privilege to have presided over such an array of talent and generosity for twenty-four exciting years.

CHAPTER TEN

Other Notable Relationships

THE FOLLOWING PARAGRAPHS OFFER BRIEF vignettes of a few more individuals who were significant in the development of the IU Jacobs School of Music and the life of the Webb family.

Dr. Jeremy Allen

Dr. Jeremy Allen is Dean of the Jacobs School of Music of Indiana University. His major field of study is jazz, and he heads one of the most distinguished university jazz degree programs in the country. The School of Music has thrived under his imaginative leadership.

Mrs. William Ball

Mrs. William Ball, a major benefactor of the school of music, invited me to her house one fall afternoon to see a concert grand Steinway piano that she was giving to the Indianapolis Symphony Orchestra. She'd had the piano delivered to her living room, where it would remain for a few weeks before being transported to the symphony concert hall.

I asked if she would like to hear the piano, and she responded with an enthusiastic yes. Among other selections, I remember playing a Liszt piano sonata. Afterwards, I commented on how lucky the Indianapolis Symphony was to receive such a gift, and Mrs. Ball immediately responded, "Well, if I'm giving a piano to the symphony, why wouldn't I give one to the IU School of Music?" I told her I could see no reason why she should not do so, and she replied, "Contact Mr. Manterfield at the bank and tell him I am giving a piano similar to the one I gave the symphony to the IU School of Music."

Next, Mrs. Ball asked me to come into her breakfast area. She opened a large walnut cabinet that contained a complete set of Meissen China with all serving dishes and service for twelve. She asked her chauffeur to find some corrugated cardboard boxes in which to transport the dishes, and when she finished boxing it up, she said to me, "I know Kenda loves this china, and I want you to take it home as a gift from me."

I couldn't believe all of this was transpiring but I did as Mrs. Ball said and presented the china to Kenda that afternoon. We were both stunned at such generosity and were able to stay in contact with Mrs. Ball until her death several years later.

Joshua Bell

Joshua Bell was born in Bloomington, Indiana, where he spent his formative years. He attended the public schools and became acquainted with the violin at an early age through Mimi Zweig's well-known string program. His rapid rise to international fame was a source of pride and great pleasure to all who knew him.

Joshua has played with every major orchestra on the globe and has been a soloist on the world's most important stages. A part-time violin faculty member of the Jacobs School of Music since 2007, he attracts students from many countries.

Dave Brubeck

Dave Brubeck is one of America's most famous jazz composers and performers. His music is performed all over the world and his recordings are legendary. I got to know him well when we served together on the faculty of a Campus at Sea academic program during the summer of 1969. One of his most famous compositions is an oratorio called *The Light in the Wilderness* written for vocal soloists, orchestra, chorus, and jazz piano. For its world premiere, he invited the First United Methodist Church choir to sing the choral parts and agreed to come to Bloomington and play the solo piano parts. I was the conductor, and it was a great experience. That piece has been performed many times all over the world.

The Cook Family

One of the "Horatio Alger" success stories of corporate and business development in the United States is the creation and rise of the William A. Cook corporation. Begun in their small apartment Bart Villa on second street in Bloomington Indiana, it has grown to become one of the nation's largest and most successful multi-national corporations.

All of this started when William Cook began manufacturing medical catheters and other devices used in surgical procedures. Mr. Cook approached surgeons about their specific needs and was able to construct instruments that satisfied the doctors' wants. From that humble beginning grew a huge network containing hundreds of corporate offices and laboratories throughout the world.

Mrs. Cook's interest in historic architecture and Carl's continuation of their philanthropic and medical discoveries broadened the scope and spread of the Cook contributions to medical and cultural development. The creation of the William and Gail Cook music library of Indiana University Jacob School of Music gave the school one of the nation's most forward-looking and complete music libraries.

The friendships and love that the Cook-Webb families share continue to this day, and we look forward to additional scientific and musical research because of their abiding interest and generosity.

Tom and Ellen Ehrlich

Tom Ehrlich was also the type of person a dean prays to have for a president. He always provided support when I needed it, he loved to savor new experiences, and he encouraged original thinking in all his actions. In addition, because he did not micromanage, I was allowed to implement my own best ideas. Kenda and I were privileged to get to know Tom and Ellen soon after they moved to Bloomington. They immediately occupied Bryan House, the President's House, but wanted some interior design changes. After considering several firms, they decided to hire Upper-Webb Interiors. This brought the two families into closer proximity than would have occurred without such a relationship. After the interior design work was finished, we continued to enjoy a close friendship and spend quality time together.

The Ehrliches were quite generous with their Bloomington house. When our son, Charlie, married, the Ehrliches invited our family from Texas to be their house guests during the wedding festivities. The morning after the wedding, they hosted a beautiful brunch on their delightful terrace.

Our friendship has lasted many years and will continue in the future as long as we are alive.

Rusty and Ann Harrison

Two long-time friends are Rusty and Ann Harrison of Attica, Indiana. Rusty served as president of Harrison Steel Company. Ann worked tirelessly raising support for Santa Fe Opera as well as lending her talents underwriting civic and cultural organizations throughout the state of Indiana. They were both generous supporters of the Jacobs School of Music and spent a great deal of time and energy encouraging and assisting outstanding young musicians who otherwise would have been unable to attend a major music school. After Rusty's death in 2017, Ann continued their philanthropic activities for many important ventures throughout the state of Indiana and indeed the United States.

Esther Kim and Joseph Kaiser

Esther Kim and Joseph Kaiser are two of the most talented students ever to attend IU Jacobs School of Music. I first became acquainted with Esther when we appeared at a concert together in her home state of California. She was twelve years old and played a difficult Mozart sonata for violin and piano. At the time she graduated from high school, in 2006, she had been flying every week from California to New York for lessons with Juilliard's famous violin professor, Dorothy Delay. When I discovered this, I persuaded her to come to Bloomington to study with one of our major violin professors. She did so, and under the direction of Jamie Laredo, she made fantastic progress.

Esther's fiancé, Joseph Kaiser, was a phenomenal cellist working with Janos Starker. One day they told me they'd always had an interest in medicine and were going to pursue a doctor of medicine degree with a focus on pediatrics. I was aghast at this news, but I knew they were brilliant students and imagined they would be successful. That is how they proceeded, and each now has a doctorate in medicine as well as advanced degrees in music.

Dr. Norman Krieger

Dr. Norman Krieger, Chairman of the Piano Department of Indiana University, is one of America's most outstanding concert pianists and music educators. He has performed a dedicatory concert on the new Steinway concert grand piano on the stage of the Main Auditorium of Indiana University, and regularly gives master classes around the world.

The Eli Lilly Family

Another extremely generous benefactor to the school of music was the Eli Lilly family, which had given one of the Lilly houses in its Indianapolis compound to Indiana University for use by scholars and guests who had business in Indianapolis. During this time, the Lillys discovered that Valentine's Day was my birthday and that Kenda was planning a party in Indianapolis. Ellen Ehrlich, the wife of the IU president, offered to have a birthday party for me in the sumptuous Lilly house. This long-remembered event was a birthday party like none I had ever before experienced.

Sylvia McNair

One of America's favorite soloists is Sylvia McNair, a world-renowned soprano who has appeared on all major concert stages and famous opera houses. Ms. McNair is a wonderful personal friend as well as a great professional colleague, and it has been an honor to perform as pianist with her on many occasions.

Charles with Sylvia McNair

Sylvia is sought after to sing leading soprano roles in many parts of the world. One of the most interesting aspects of her concert work is her ability to sing favorite concert and operatic repertoire and to follow that with impassioned renderings of leading Broadway show tunes.

Several years ago, Sylvia and I performed a concert in Dallas, Texas, as part of the Highlander Concert Series of Highland Park Presbyterian Church. Olin Chism, major critic for the *Dallas Morning News*, said on that occasion, "Ms. McNair's striking program made it seem worthwhile to be inside on one of the season's loveliest afternoons." Mr. Chism went on to praise Sylvia's vocal English diction by saying, "Ms. McNair could give lessons in singing the language clearly. No printed text was needed."

Dr. Michael McRobbie

Dr. Michael McRobbie, President of Indiana University, has been a strong supporter of the Jacobs School of Music throughout his tenure as President. The Jacobs School continues to be the largest school of music associated with a major university in the United States.

Irwin and Xenia Miller

Irwin and Xenia Miller of Columbus, Indiana, were some of the most influential and generous patrons of the Jacobs School of Music. For many years, Irwin was CEO of Cummins Engine Corporation. During his stint with that major corporation, it became one of the leading engine builders in the world. Irwin and Xenia were both extremely interested in twentieth-century architecture and funded outstanding architectural drawings for homes and buildings throughout Columbus and the surrounding area. I had a wonderful opportunity to get to know Xenia as we were both named to the Indiana Governor's Arts Commission for two consecutive four-year terms.

During this time, Irwin was also a member of the Ford Foundation Board, and he spoke to me about his interest in having one of the foundation's annual meetings in Columbus so that he could show the foundation members the wonders of Columbus architecture. He was successful in arranging a meeting and a dinner for the group at the Miller home. He called me to invite a student musical group to entertain the guests and asked that a violinist, cellist, and pianist perform Tschaikowsky's "Piano Trio."

We chose Yuval Yaron on the violin, Gary Hoffman on cello, and Shigeo Neriki on piano, all three of whom have gone on to stellar professional careers. They did a great job, and afterward Irwin talked to the trio and asked Yuval what kind of violin he had played. Yuval responded, "Oh, it's nothing. It's an Israeli instrument I brought with me." Mr. Miller then asked, "Have you ever played a Stradivarius violin?"

"Why no," Yuval replied. "Where would I find a Stradivarius to play?"

Mr. Miller went back to his bedroom and returned with a beautiful case that held two violins. He opened the case and said, "I also play the violin. Not nearly as well as you do, but I own two Stradivarius violins and keep them in excellent condition. Pick one and play it if you like."

Yuval carefully removed one of the violins from the case and began to play. In about thirty seconds, he began to cry and said, "The violin is like an extension of my arm. It is playing itself." The entire group was moved to tears.

Another slightly less elevating memory that involved the Millers occurred a few days before Christmas. Both Kenda and Xenia were avid collectors of Christmas manger scenes. In her lifetime, Kenda amassed approximately sixty sets that included the holy family, shepherds, livestock, and wise men. Kenda had invited the Millers for supper, and as we walked into the dining room, she let out a shriek. I quickly looked around and was shocked to see that someone had "mounted" all the animals in compromising positions. As I surveyed the faces of our four boys, it became painfully obvious that Malcolm was the perpetrator.

Kenda gathered herself, calmly walked to the dining room table, and rearranged all the animals exactly as she had originally placed them. Fortunately, the Millers had a good sense of humor, and after some laughter, we proceeded to have a delicious dinner.

Gwyn and Barbara Richards

I first met Gwyn Richards when he was a student in the choral conducting program at the IU School of Music. While still a graduate student, his abilities, both in music and administration, were noticed by numerous faculty and students. However, before finishing his degree, he was siphoned away to become an assistant dean of the school of music at Rice University. He later became an assistant dean at the University of Southern California.

We invited him back as Director of Admissions for the IU School of Music, where he served closely with me on the administrative committee. From there he was appointed Assistant Dean and ultimately Dean of the IU Jacobs School of Music. For twenty years, he served with great success and distinction before retiring in 2020. We also served together with much happiness at First United Methodist Church in Bloomington as choir director and organist.

Our professional life was always a joy for me, and our families became closer in succeeding years. Barbara, Gwyn's wife, was a part of our family from the beginning. An educator in her own right, Barbara influenced countless lives teaching reading recovery to children in the Monroe County school system. Megan and Jillian, their daughters, their respective sons-in-law, Austin and Andrew, and their five grandchildren complement our vacations and wonderful family gatherings with humor, excitement, and love.

Marianne Williams Tobias

Marianne Williams Tobias is a member of the Friends of Music and has given tremendous support to the Indiana University Jacobs School of Music. She helped edit The Art of Descant book written by Charles.

Dr. and Mrs. William Turner

Dr. William Turner served on the faculty of the IU Medical School. I was first introduced to him by my son, Kent, who had Dr. Turner as a professor of surgery at the University of Texas Southwestern Medical Center in Dallas before he accepted his appointment as chairman of the department of surgery at Methodist Hospital in Indianapolis. A devoted teacher, Dr. Turner was deeply involved with Methodist Hospital's merger with the IU Medical Center.

Kent was enormously enthusiastic about his classes with Dr. Turner and was anxious for the two families to meet. Upon meeting, we discovered the Turners were great lovers of classical music and attended many concerts given by faculty and students. During that time, we spent meaningful hours together and became close friends.

During Kenda's illness, both Dr. and Mrs. Turner were extremely helpful in finding emergency medical assistance. Dr. Turner was well-known for his personal attention to his patients, and those who were assigned to him for treatment were always deeply grateful for his attention. The Turners were also extremely supportive of the IU School of Medicine and very generous with material gifts. They are the kind of patrons all musicians dream about.

Henry and Celicia Upper

The Henry Upper family has been an integral part of the Webb family for many years. I first met Henry when I returned to SMU after my Air Force duty. There I became an assistant to Dean Orville Borchers and met up again with Kenda, who had entered SMU as a freshmen student. During that year, Henry and I became friends, first as piano accompanists for Dean Borchers' University Chorale and later as fellow students in the piano doctoral program at IU.

On June 21, 1958, Kenda and I married and immediately moved to Bloomington, where Dr. Borchers had advised Henry to pursue a doctorate in piano. Fred Waring appointed Henry to the faculty of his choral workshops, and Dean Bain appointed him to the faculty of IU. When I became Dean he was appointed Assistant Dean. Capable of solving difficult problems, his advice and influence were highly respected and sought after.

Henry brought his bride, Celicia, to Bloomington, and they quickly became part of our family. They had one child, Andy, a remarkable human being who had both physical and mental disabilities that did not deter him from becoming a beloved and integral part of our family.

Celicia was the other half of Upper-Webb Interiors, and she and Kenda formed the closest of ties. They provided the interior design to more than seven hundred residential and commercial enterprises throughout the state of Indiana.

Herman B Wells

Herman B Wells has undoubtedly had more influence in the long history of Indiana University than any other single individual. He served as president or chancellor for sixty years and regarded IU as his family. Dr. Wells loved music, and on many occasions I found him sitting alone in the Musical Arts Center, Auer Hall, or a smaller facility drinking in the music being performed.

One specific occasion made a powerful impression on me. As I was walking into Auer Hall one evening for a choral concert, I met Dr. Wells walking into a balcony seat. We greeted each other, and he said, "Charles, I want to hear this whole concert, but I have a meeting I must attend at 9:15; therefore, I will have to miss the last part of the concert." I told him I certainly understood and that I was glad he was able to come at all.

After the concert was over and I was walking to my car, I saw Dr. Wells also leaving Auer Hall. I remarked that he'd said he had to leave at 9:15, and he replied, "Yes, that was my plan, but the music was so beautiful I just couldn't leave."

Herman Wells was a great supporter of the school of music in all its endeavors. He was thrilled with the New York City undertakings, especially with the fact that we could mount a full-scale opera in the Metropolitan Opera House. Any dean would be overjoyed to work for such a president.

Camilla Williams

Camilla Williams has been a voice faculty member of IU Jacobs School of Music since 1977. She was the first African-American to sing a non-traditional black role in New York City, performing the role of Butterfly in Puccini's opera *Madama Butterfly*.

Ms. Williams sang concerts throughout the United States, and I had the privilege of performing with her on numerous occasions, including at the Democratic Governors Association annual meeting chaired by President William Clinton in Washington, D. C.

Virginia Zeani and Nicola Rossi-Lemeni

In 1980, I appointed Virginia Zeani and her husband, Nicola Rossi-Lemeni, to the voice faculty of the school of music. Both had been brilliant singers in their native countries and had enjoyed superb careers in their chosen fields. They immediately attracted outstanding students to their studios and became some of the most sought-after teachers on the faculty. Upon the death of her husband, Virginia moved to Florida and was unable to continue teaching for us. It was a great loss, but I am pleased that we remain in contact and that she occasionally agrees to teach a master class in Bloomington.

APPENDIX A

Music Faculty Members with Whom I Served

Following is a list of every individual who served on the IU music school faculty during the time I was dean. As I mentioned earlier, the quality of the faculty is the single most important factor in developing an internationally recognized institution. We searched the world to find the most capable people in their various fields to appoint to this group. It is a pleasure to recognize the following members of the faculty of the Indiana University Jacobs School of Music as the largest and most brilliant collection of such people anywhere.

A

Abbenes, Arie

Abeles, Harold

Adam, William

Adelstein, Bernard

Aiken, David

Allen, Ross

Amato, Bruno

Anderson, Edwin

Anderson, Linda

Apel, Willi

Appelman, D. Ralph

Arad, Atar

Aronoff, Kenny

Arroyo, Martina

Arvin, Gary

Auer, Edward

B

Bailey, Darrell

Bain, Wilfred C.

Baker, Claude

Baker, David

Baldner, Thomas

Baldwin, Fredrick S. Jr.

Baldwin, Marcia

Balkwill, Bryan

Barlow, Klara

Bates, Earl

Battersby, Edmund

Bayless, Eugene

Beach, Phillip

Belnap, Michael

Bennett, Alan

Beriozoff, Nicolas

Berman, Boris

Béroff, Michel

Beversdorf, S. Thomas

Binkley, Thomas

Birmingham, Hugh Jr.

Biss, Paul

Bitetti, Ernesto

Block, Michel

Bloom, Myron

Boepple, Hans

Bolet, Jorge

Bonnefoux, Jean-Pierre

Boszorményi-Nagy, Béla

Bowles, Kenneth

Brancart, Evelyne

Bransby, Bruce

Brenner, Brenda

Bricht, Walter

Bristow, Alice

Brown, A. Peter

Brown, Keith

Brown, Malcolm

Buelow, George

Burkholder, J. Peter

Burns, Stephen

Burrows, Elmar

Busch, Hans

Buswell, James O. IV

C

Calder, George

Campbell, James

Carlyss, Gerald

Cassel, Walter

Caswell, Austin

Cavallo-Gulli, Enrica

Cesbron, Jacques

Cesbron, Virginia

Christ, William

Clark, Mark Ross

Colón, Emilio

Contino, Fiora

Cord, Edmund

Cordero, Roque

Corra, Arthur

Covington, Kate

Cramer, Ray

Cristini, C. Mario

Cuccaro, Constanza

D

Dahl, Ole Steffen

d'Angelo, Gianna

Daniel, Ralph

Davidson, Louis

Davies, Dudley

Davis, Agnes

Davy, Gloria

Dean, Allan

Deis, Jean

deLerma, Domonique-René

DeLone, Richard Pierre

Denk, Jeremy

de Pasquale, Joseph

deVeritch, Alan

Dimitrov, Antonin

Dolin, Anton

Dubinsky, Luba Edlina

Dubinsky, Rostislav

Duffin, Gerald

Dunn, Thomas

Dzubay, David

E

Eagle, Peter

Eaton, John

Eban, Eli

Ebbs, Fredrick

Effron, David

Elliott, Paul

Elvira, Pablo Jr.

Elworthy, Robert

England, Wilber

Erb, Donald

Erdelyi, Csaba

Esposito, Giovanni

Evans, Lucile

Evans, Robert

F

Farbman, Edith

Farbman, Harry

Farkas, Philip

Farrell, Eileen

Felberg, Leonard

Fenske, David

Fiorillo, Marcia

Fleming–May, Lissa

Fosha, Leon

Foster, Bronja

Foster, Sidney

Fox, Frederick

Freund, Donald

Fried, Miriam

Fuerstner, Carl

Fuks, Mauricio

Fulcher, Jane

G

Gaber, George

Gass, Glenn

Gelvin, Miriam

Gersten, Frederick

Gersten, Joan

Gilfoy, Jack

Gillespie, Wendy

Gingold, Josef

Glidden, Robert

Goetze, Mary

Gordon, Michael

Gorham, Charles

Graef, Richard

Graf, Hans

Green, Barry

Gregory, Ronald

Grinstead, Montana

Grist, Reri

Grodner, Murray

Guilet, Daniel

Gulick, Henry

Gulli, Franco

H

Hall, Marion

Hancock, Jory

Haney, Lewis Van

Harbison, Patrick

Harler, Alan

Harrington, Jan

Harris, Roy

Harshaw, Margaret

Hart, Mary Ann

Hartman, Scott

Hass, Jeffrey

Hasty, D. Stanley

Hatfield, Michael

Hatten, Robert

Havranek, Patricia

Havranek, Roger

Heiden, Bernhard

Heifetz, Benar

Herford, Julius

Herz, Gerhard

Higgins, C. David

Hillier, Paul L.

Hillis, Margaret

Hoffer, Charles

Hoffman, Gary

Hoffzimmer, Ernest

Hokanson, Leonard

Holloway, Clyde

Horlacher, Gretchen

Horner, Jerry

Hornibrook, W. Wallace

Houdeshel, Harry F. Jr.

Houser, W. Roy

Howell, John

Hurst, Lawrence

Husch, Gerhard

I

Ik-Hwan Bae

Ilmer, Irving

Isaacson, Eric

Izquierdo, Juan Pablo

J

Jackson, Wayne

Janzer, Eva Czako

Janzer, Georges

Jensen, Wilma

Jeter, John

Johnson, Hugh B. Jr

Johnson, Richard

Jones, Ted

Jorgensen, Estelle

K

Kallaur, Barbara

Kashkashian, Kim

Kaufmann, Freda

Kaufmann, Walter

Keiser, Marilyn

Kelley, Dorothy

Kent, Charles

Kielian-Gilbert, Marianne

Kiesgen, Paul

King, James

Kliewer, Vernon

Klotman, Robert

Klug, Howard

Knoll, Richard

Kogan, Pavel

Kowalski, Henryk

Kozma, Tibor

Krajewska, Marian

Krueger, George

Kubiak, Teresa

Kullman, Charles

Kuttner, Michael

L

Lazan, Albert

Legêne, Eva

Lifschey, Marc

Liotta, Vincent

Lipton, Martha

List, George

Long, Newell

Lucas, James

Lucas, Michael

Luciano, Lynn

Ludwig, Gunther

Lukas, Kathryn

M

McBride, Patricia

McDonald, Susann

McGreer, Dennis

Mack, Harold

MacWatters, Virginia

Madison, Thurber

Magee, Jeffrey

Magg, Fritz

Magg, Natasha

Manski, Dorothee

Mannion, Elizabeth

Masselos, William

Mathiesen, Thomas

Matthen, Paul

Melville, Kenneth

Merker, Ethel

Miedema, Harry

Milanov, Zinka

Miller, Eleanor Gough

Montané, Carlos

Montecino, Alfonso

Moore, Dale

Moses, Don

Mueller, Herbert

N

Nagosky, John

Naoumoff, Émile

Neriki, Shigeo

Nettl, Gertrud

Nettl, Paul

Neumeyer, David

Newman, Anthony

Noble, Timothy

Noblitt, Thomas

Nolting, Betty Ferris

Nomikos, Andreas

O

O'Brien, Eugene

O'Hearn, Robert

Ogdon, John

Orrego-Salas, Juan

P

Pagels, Jurgen

Pal, Tridib

Palló, Imre

Paskevska, Anna V.

Peck, Leslie

Pellerite, James

Pemberton, Roger Max

Penhorwood, Edwin

Perantoni, Daniel

Perlemuter, Vlado

Phan, Phuc Q.

Phelps, Mark

Phillips, Harvey

Phillips, Leonard

Pickett, David

Porco, Robert

Portnoy, Bernard

Potter, Gary

Pratt, Stephen

Pressler, Menahem

Primrose, William

R

Ragatz, Oswald

Rayfield, Robert

Reed, Gilbert

Rehm, John

Reisberg, Horace

Reyes, Alberto

Reynolds, Verne

Rezits, Joseph

Ricci, Ruggiero

Richards, Gwyn

Ritchie, Stanley

Rivera, Benito

Roach, George

Robert, Walter

Robertello, Thomas

Roberts, William

Rodman, Fontaine

Rolf, Marie

Rommel, John

Rosenberg, Sidney

Rosenberg, Sylvia

Ross, Allan

Ross, William

Rossi, Urico

Rossi-Lemeni, Nicola

Röthlisberger, Max

Rothmuller, Marko

Rousseau, Eugene

Rowell, Lewis

Royce, Anya

Rudnytsky, Roman

S

Sabline, Oleg

Sadlo, Milos

St. Leger, Frank

Samuelsen, Roy

Sandström, Sven-David

Sankey, Stuart

Scammon, Vera

Schillin, Scott

Schleuter, Stanley

Schmidt, Charles

Scholz, Gottfried

Schwartzkopf, Michael

Scott, James

Sears, William

Sebok, Gyorgy

Seraphinoff, Richard

Shapiro, Laurence

Sharrow, Leonard

Shaver, Stephen

Shaw, Karen

Shkolnikova, Nelli

Shriner, C. William

Simon, Abbey

Sinor, Eugenia

Sirucek, Jerry

Skernick, Abraham

Skolovsky, Zadel

Smith, Carol

Smith, Henry Charles

Smith, Larry

Snyder, Richard

Snygg, Fran

Sollberger, Harvey

Sollors, Daniel

Solomon, Izler

Spada, Pietro

Sparks, Thomas

Spera, Dominic

Spezialé, Marie

Stahl, Edwin

Starker, Janos

Starkey, Evelyn Saxton

Stedman, W. Preston

Steele, Nancy

Stewart, Lila

Stewart, M. Dee

Stewart, Val

Stoll, Robert

Stowell, Richard

Strong, Douglas

Svetlova, Marina

Szmyt, Elzbieta

T

Takahashi, Yuji

Tangeman, Robert

Taylor, Karen

Taylor, Myron

Téllez, Carmen

Teraspulsky, Leopold

Thomson, William

Tischler, Hans

Tocco, James

Tong Il Han

Tozzi, Giorgio

Tsutsumi, Tsuyoshi

Tucci, Gabriella

Turkovic, Milan

U

Umeyama, Shuichi

Upper, Henry

V

Vacano, Wolfgang

Van Buskirk, Carl

Vanderbeke, Patricia

Vaszonyi, Balint

Verdy, Violette

Vitale, Vincenzo

Vlassenko, Lev

W

Walker, Kim

Walsh, Daniel

Walsh, Thomas

Watson, Jack

Webb, Charles H. Jr.

Weisz, Robert

Wennerstrom, Mary

Wesner-Hoehn, Beverly

White, Allen

White, John R.

White, Margaret Buehler

Will, Roy

Williams, Camilla

Wilson, George

Wincene, Carole

Winold, C. Allen

Winold, Helga

Wise, Patricia

Wittlich, Gary

Wood, Linda

Wood, Richard

Wood, Thomas

Woodley, David

Woods, David G.

Wright, Elisabeth

Wronski, Tadeusz

Wustman, John

X

Xenakis, Iannis

APPENDIX B

Awards

I present this next section with a disclaimer, by which I mean I am uncomfortable speaking about my own honors. However, I have been advised that this information is part of the whole story; therefore, I include it without comment or further explanation.

Distinguished Service Medal, United States Air Force, 1956

Sagamore of the Wabash, awarded in 1980, 1981, and 1997 by the state of Indiana; Kenda also received this award in 1997

Distinguished Alumnus, Highland Park High School, 1989

Living Legend of Indiana, State of Indiana, 2004

Distinguished Alumnus, Southern Methodist University, 1980

Marquis Who's Who in America, 2000; Kenda also received this award in 2001

Honorary member Alliance of Distinguished Rank Professors, Indiana University, 1997

Distinguished Alumni Service Award, Indiana University, June 2005

Named a Member of the Indiana Academy, 1983

President's Medal for Excellence, Indiana University, 2000

Governor's Arts Award, State of Indiana, 1989

Hendl Award, Dallas Symphony Orchestra, 1949

Thomas Hart Benton Mural Medallion, Indiana University, 1987

Webb–Ehrlich Great Organ of Alumni Hall, named in honor of Charles and Kenda Webb and Thomas and Ellen Ehrlich for their distinguished service to Indiana University, June 2013

The Herald-Telephone Wednesday, December 21, 1988

IU music dean to get Governor's Arts Award

Associated Press

INDIANAPOLIS — Indiana University Music School Dean Charles Webb will be presented the 1989 Indiana Governor's Arts Award for arts educators.

The 1989 arts award for professional artists will go to jazz trombonist J.J. Johnson and interior designer Mark Hampton.

Gov. Robert D. Orr announced Tuesday that the three men will be among six recipients when the awards are presented at a Feb. 7 ceremony in the Statehouse rotunda.

Other recipients will be Eli Lilly and Co., winner of the corporate award; the city of Evansville, city award, and Harrison Eiteljorg of Indianapolis, arts patron award.

"They have helped create our modern culture with their artistry and their leadership in the arts," Orr said of the recipients.

The arts awards have been presented every other year since 1973. Past winners have included the novelist Kurt Vonnegut Jr., novelist and screenwriter Steve Tesich, designer Bill Blass, composers Hoagy Carmichael and Cole Porter, artist Robert Indiana, Cummins Engine Co. and the city of Jasper.

The awards are sponsored by the Indiana Arts Commission, Indiana Advocates for the Arts and the Indiana Endowment for the Arts.

Webb, dean of the world's largest music school since 1973, was cited for his efforts to attract internationally prominent faculty and to train artists and educators who become leaders in their field. In addition to his administrative duties in Bloomington, Webb is also an accomplished pianist and conductor.

Johnson, an Indianapolis resident, is a trombonist and composer credited with revolutionizing jazz trombone playing. A pioneer of the bebop era, he performed with the orchestras of Benny Carter and Count Basie and worked with jazz greats such as Miles Davis, Charlie Parker and Dizzy Gillespie.

Johnson and fellow trombonist Kai Winding also led their own quintet. Johnson recently completed a world tour with his new quintet.

A New York City resident originally from Plainfield, Hampton established his own design firm in 1975 and has gained an international reputation for his work in restoration of important buildings and interior design.

Among his projects were the official residence of the vice president in Washington, D.C., the New York City mayor's residence and the Metropolitan Museum of Art in New York.

Eli Lilly, the Indianapolis-based pharmaceutical company, donated more than $1 million to cultural organizations including arts groups during 1987, according to the governor's office. The company also has a matching gift program to encourage its employees and retirees to donate to cultural groups.

Evansville, Orr's hometown, was cited for its commitment to encouraging the development of the arts through the expenditure of city funds and the presentation of the annual mayor's arts awards. The city also committed $15,000 toward a fee for a consultant to assess the

Herald Times news clipping, 1988

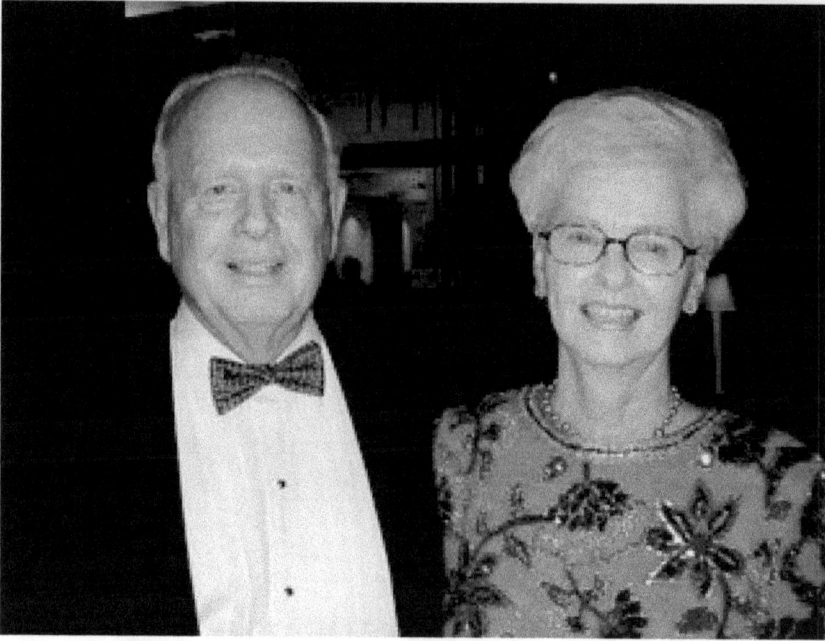

Charles and Nancy at an awards dinner in Indianapolis

As a parting gift, please enjoy videos of Charles by searching 'Charles Webb at his Piano'
on https://www.youtube.com,
or via this URL address: https://lnkd.in/gJpZVQj

www.ingramcontent.com/pod-product-compliance
Lightning Source LLC
Chambersburg PA
CBHW080538090426

42733CB00016B/2620